the series on school reform

Patricia A. Wasley
University
of Washington

Ann Lieberman
Senior Scholar,
Stanford University

Joseph P. McDonald
New York
University

SERIES EDITORS

(Continued)

the series on school reform, *continued*

What
Should
I Do?

Confronting Dilemmas of
Teaching in Urban Schools

Anna Ershler Richert

Teachers College, Columbia University
New York and London

Published by Teachers College Press, 1234 Amsterdam Avenue, New York, NY 10027

Library of Congress Cataloging-in-Publication Data

Richert, Anna Ershler.
What should I do? : confronting dilemmas of teaching in urban schools / Anna Ershler
  Richert.
    p. cm. — (Series on school reform)
   ISBN 978-0-8077-5325-5 (pbk. : alk. paper)
    1. Teaching—United States. 2. Urban schools—United States. I. Title.
   LB1025.3.R5345 2012
   371.102—dc23   2011049155

ISBN 978-0-8077-5325-5 (paperback)
Printed on acid-free paper

Manufactured in the United States of America

19 18 17 16 15 14 13 12 8 7 6 5 4 3 2 1

For Irving and Eunice Ershler, who started me on this journey;
Alfred Jacobs, who encouraged me along the way;
and the Oakland and East Bay teachers, whose determination
and hard work continue to inspire me every day.

Contents

Series Foreword

There have been hundreds of books written about teachers—who they are, what they should do, how they should behave, what they should know. . . . But there are few that get inside the real *practice* of teaching as Anna Richert's book does in *What Should I Do?* This is a book not only for new teachers, but for all of us who care about teaching and learning in under-resourced schools.

This book is a partnership between a great teacher, Richert, and her students who write about their teaching dilemmas while learning to teach. The book reads like a marvelous detective story where we follow the many dilemmas that novice teachers' face along with the sage and gentle teaching that Richert facilitates in helping these brave and committed teachers learn that there are problems to be *solved*, but numerous dilemmas that must be *managed*.

We learn that many of these dilemmas are only faced in the experience of actual teaching and that part of learning to teach is figuring out how to anticipate what to do when one is confronted by moral dilemmas for which there are no easy answers.

Richert sifts her way through scores of dilemma narratives that she has collected over the years with her students and finds that in the particulars of teaching in urban contexts, there are themes that keep reappearing. There is the struggle for professional identity, which both "shapes" and "challenges" the way teachers think of themselves. There are dilemmas about student/teacher relationships that present both racial and class differences where teachers are called upon to balance the needs of individuals as well as those of groups. There are dilemmas in the content of what should be taught, as these novice teachers work hard to connect school content to their students' lives. In the process, students connect to *their* questions and *their* experiences, which are often different from their teachers. What should the teachers do in these circumstances? As in all of teaching, novices need to somehow evaluate and make judgments of what their students are learning. And again, we struggle with these teachers as, in some cases, students need to take tests where they don't know the language; where teachers learn about the difficulties of their student's lives that place limits on their studying—yet they must make assessments about their students' learning.

Richert is there helping all of us understand that values and beliefs must be considered along with one's professional and moral judgments. At last we get a book that gets inside the real situations and complexities of urban schools. We learn as we try to better understand the experience of teachers, as they reveal to us authentic stories and dilemmas of their prac-tice. We are moved by the students' stories as well as the sensitive strug-gles of their teachers and the reasoned and deep discussion by Richert. This is the kind of teacher and teacher educator we need and the kind of book we need to educate us about the realities of urban schools and what it means to be a good teacher.

—Ann Lieberman, Senior Scholar at Stanford University

Acknowledgments

Like everything else I know, this book is a reflection of many years of talking and working with friends, colleagues, and students. To all of them I owe much gratitude. There are some who warrant singling out because the particular book project would not have been possible without them. First, I owe special thanks to the teachers whose dilemma narratives are included here. Not only have they shared their work generously with me, they have offered to share it with whomever happens upon and reads this book. They are joined by hundreds of other former students, now teachers, whose work also informed this project. Their energy and commitment have propelled the effort forward.

My colleagues at Mills have been my sounding board throughout this project—and all others. Thank you Vicki LaBoskey, Linda Kroll, Tomás Galguera, Ruth Cossey, and Dave Donahue. Pam Grossman and Suzanne Wilson, my original writing partners, have provided decades of steadfast support. Lee Shulman, who is never too busy to talk with me about whatever is on my mind, has taught me among other things that being a dissertation advisor is a lifelong commitment. I owe him much thanks.

Early in the analysis of the dilemma cases, I received the thoughtful engagement of Jen Corn, Colette Rabin, Rachel Siegel, and Kristi Leunig, who got me on track and kept me there. Lynn Holm nudged me to start this work and has been a supporter ever since. Dave Donahue, my colleague and writing partner, read the book, chapter by chapter, and provided invaluable feedback and support throughout the project. Claire Bove also read pieces of the work and provided wonderful feedback at the perfect moment. Linda Kroll provided a beautiful spot for a writing retreat and much support for the project as well.

I am grateful for the constant encouragement and support from my friend and colleague Ann Lieberman, who invited me to contribute to her series, to Marie Ellen Larcada, my TC Press editor, whose kind and quick responses to my questions reduced any anxiety that surfaced along the way, and to Jennifer Baker, who stepped in to guide the project through the production stage providing much thoughtful advice and patient guidance as the project drew to a close. Leslie Mariska Neill brought her careful eye and good spirit to tie up the formatting loose ends, which was a great help. And Marilyn, whose belief in this work and in me—along with a steady supply of encouragement (and fresh coffee)—made the completion of the book possible. I wouldn't be at the acknowledgment-writing stage had she not been on board with me throughout.

This project began with the gift of one month's time at a writing retreat in Bellagio, Italy, sponsored by the Rockefeller Foundation. There at the Villa Serbionne, I was able—as I had never been before nor have I since—to stop and think deeply and carefully about my work and what I have learned from doing it. For that I am profoundly grateful.

Introduction

For 2 decades or more I have collected and read ethical dilemma cases written by my graduate students who are learning to teach in urban schools. With every new set, I am bowled over by the honesty, intelligence, and courage of these novice professionals. I am also humbled by the brave determination of their students and their students' families, who live in the urban metropolitan center where their children go to school and where my students and I work. The dilemma narratives have provided me a privileged window into the realities of the urban school experience for teachers and the processes involved in learning to teach in this vibrant and yet challenging setting. Every year I read a new set of cases, and every year I am determined to find a way to share them with others. As I have said to my students over the years, someone other than my mother, who is over 80 years old, and me needs to read their accounts. This book is my attempt at sharing this work beyond my mother's living room.

The book focuses on the challenges of teaching and learning to teach in urban schools. It's based on the premise that teaching and learning to teach are context specific. Whereas in many ways teaching is teaching—and teachers across contexts share things in common—there are also characteristics of different settings that require a different framing of the work. Teaching in an urban school presents challenges that are unlike those facing teachers in a rural or even a nearby suburban community. My goal in writing the book was to look closely at the connection between dilemmas teachers predictably encounter in their work, and the setting where the work takes place. I wanted to see if I could better understand what it means—and what it takes—to teach and to learn to teach in urban schools.

To tackle these questions I sorted out from a collection of more than 300 teaching dilemmas those that were in some way connected to the urban-school context. My analyses of those dilemmas generated a set of characteristics of the urban setting that predictably challenge newcomers and veteran teachers alike. It also generated a set of four categories into which the dilemmas fall: dilemmas about professional identity; dilemmas about caring for students; dilemmas about what and how to teach; and dilemmas about assessing student learning. I believe that teachers in all settings confront dilemmas in these four areas of teaching. But for this book I focused on the intersection of the urban setting and its impact on these central components of the work.

The book includes a discussion of 22 of these dilemma narratives as they clustered into the four theme areas. The teachers' narratives are interwoven with my analysis of them. My hope is that the book's readers will contemplate the two perspectives on the dilemmas presented (the teacher's and mine) and offer additional perspectives making the case richer each time. Like the dilemmas themselves that by definition have no "right" or "wrong" answer or resolution, the analysis of these cases is not presented as a definitive understanding of the case. I realize that I bring to this work my perspective as a White female teacher educator with a set of experiences all of which influence my interpretation of the events the teachers describe. My purpose as a reader and interpreter, therefore, is to begin an "conversation" with other readers who will share their interpretations of these narrative dilemma texts. My goal was not to judge the cases, but to understand the teaching they describe. I invite other readers to do the same and, in their conversations about them, contribute to an expanded interpretation of the issues they raise regarding the work of urban schools. The more perspectives we entertain about the complexities of teaching and learning in this setting, the more likely it is that we can find ways to better support both teachers and students who spend their precious days in the context of the urban classroom.

THE BOOK'S STRUCTURE

In his classic essay, *The Practical 4*, Joseph Schwab (1983) suggested four teaching "commonplaces"—the teacher, the student, the content, and the milieu. The dilemma categories discussed in the chapters that follow cluster into Schwab's commonplaces. Chapter 2 addresses the category of teacher. In this chapter we find dilemmas that have to do with professional identity and authority. They reveal the novices' struggle to develop a professional identity as teacher, including the need to embrace the role and assume authority in the classroom. Chapter 3 includes dilemmas that focus on students—in particular, dilemmas that arise from the teacher's challenges to establish and maintain caring student-teacher relationships that are positive and productive. In this category are also cases that reveal the teacher's struggle to define the qualities and boundaries of the student-teacher relationship. Chapters 4 and 5 cover Schwab's commonplace of content. Chapter 4 focuses on curriculum and instruction and includes dilemmas concerning what to teach and, subsequently, how to teach it. Chapter 5 turns the focus toward assessment and the myriad dilemmas urban teachers face in determining how to assess what their students know and can do. Chapter 6 steps back to consider the value of conceptualizing the work of teaching to be, in part, the managing of dilemmas, which the chapter argues makes teaching moral work as well as professional work. The chapter posits that the dilemmas facing teachers in urban schools are more predictable than we might have imagined and suggests how we might take advantage of this predictability by drawing on both the dilemma categories and case examples included in this text.

Schwab's (1983) fourth commonplace, the milieu, is central to this conceptualization. The milieu, or context, of the teaching we are considering in all of the chapters of this book is the urban school, which includes such contextual factors as: high levels of racial, cultural, and language diversity that characterize urban classrooms; the complexity of children's lives including poverty, violence, and citizenship status; and under-resourcing of schools, which often leads to poor academic preparation and low expectations. The dilemma cases included in the book reflect characteristics of the urban context that raise questions for teachers about how to act in the best interest of their students. The argument is that teaching and learning happen in a context and that context matters for both doing and understanding the work. Learning to manage the predictable dilemmas of teaching in urban schools is what this book is about.

CHAPTER 1

What Should I Do?
Managing Teaching Dilemmas

Teaching is hard work. So hard, in fact, that it takes a lifetime to learn to do it well. One reason it's so hard is because of the uncertainty of the work. Everyday—all the time—teachers encounter problems that are not easily solvable. Consider the problem described below by Ruth, for example, my former student who at the time was preparing to become a teacher. Ruth wrote this brief description of a situation she encountered in her student teaching so that she could share it with her colleagues.[1] Her hope was that they would help her reason out what steps to take with her student Carlito.

> I student teach first grade at Como Elementary School in a working class neighborhood. . . . Carlito is a Latino boy and he is the biggest kid in the class. He is very sweet and caring, but he is clearly negotiating what it means to have a "tough guy" image—he wears big chains, and sometimes will talk back, using inappropriate language that he thinks is funny. Carlito misses a great deal of school and this is unfortunate because he is in the lowest reading group in the class.
>
> One morning, Carlito asked me to come to his desk so he could tell me a story. Students have been practicing a method of using their fingers to help them tell and remember stories. I put up my five fingers (one for each point in the narrative) to help Carlito keep track of his story, and here's what he told me:
>
>> Yesterday I was driving with my brother and my brother's friends in the car. We saw a Black dude on the street with his backpack unzipped. My brother said, "You should tell him his backpack is broken," and I got out of the car and snuck up behind him and

yelled "Hey dude your backpack is messed up!" He was so scared
because I yelled it at him. I got back in the car and my brother
was laughing and said, "That's the first Black dude that was ever
scared of a White dude!"

Ruth was taken aback by Carlito's story. She wondered what she
should do. She wrote, "I didn't know what to say about the story right
away. I wanted to give Carlito positive feedback for being engaged and for
having done what we asked in terms of describing a small moment." At
the same time, she was concerned about the content of Carlito's tale. She
decided to begin by complimenting him on his clear focus: "Wow, Carlito,
I really like how your story focused in on a small moment." She continued, "I also remember noting that he'd made use of dialogue." Shifting to
a response about the content of his story she asked "if he had been *trying*
to scare the man with the backpack." Carlito said yes he did want to scare
the man because "it was so funny." Ruth expressed her concern: "'Hmm,'
I said, 'I really wouldn't like it if someone sneaked up on me like that and
then laughed about it afterward. That would feel so bad to me.'"
Ruth reported that Carlito "smiled uncomfortably" when he heard her
reaction. Given this she decided to move on with the writing lesson rather
than pursue her concern about his behavior. She did not want to discourage him from continuing to write, which she feared might happen if she
continued asking him about the incident. Unresolved about whether or not
she had done the "right" thing, she explained, "The question for me here
was how to prioritize my desire to capitalize on Carlito's unusual interest in
writing, and my desire to help him see his behavior in a critical light." She
asked her colleagues, "What should I have done?"

SOLVING TEACHING PROBLEMS

Moment to moment, teachers encounter circumstances like this—problems that are not easily solvable and yet they require action by the teacher. Some argue that these problems are not solvable at all but rather they
are dilemmas that defy clear resolution. Cuban (2001) helps by delineat-
ing a distinction between dilemmas and problems. He describes problems
as situations "in which a gap is found between what *is* and what '*ought to
be*'" (p. 4). He argues that practitioners can typically solve problems by

following procedures and routines built into the classrooms and school systems where they work. For example, fixing a broken copy machine is a problem that can be solved. Most likely it will involve contacting the person in charge of maintenance who will make arrangements for the repairperson to do the work. Problems that can be solved with these somewhat technical solutions Cuban refers to as "tame." He contrasts tame problems with others that are "wicked."

Wicked problems, according to Cuban (2001), "are ill-defined, ambiguous, complicated, interconnected situations packed with potential conflict" (p. 10). Drawing on Cuban's definition of problems as situations that can be "solved," we can think of situations that are the opposite— not solvable—as dilemmas. Teaching dilemmas are situations that require teachers to make a decision for which there is no easy or "right" answer. More often than not, they pit two or more values or goals against one another. Burbules (1997) describes a teaching dilemma:

> Not just a difficult choice between two options, not just a balancing act between alternatives, not just second-guessing a decision we might have made differently, but a recognition of deep, intractable contradiction between competing aims and values. (p. 2)

Ruth's struggle to decide whether to pursue her conversation with Carlito about his intention "to scare someone to impress his brothers and make them laugh" or to let that go temporarily so as not to discourage him from continuing with writing his story is a good example of a teaching dilemma. She was conflicted between her desire to "not shut him down" on the one hand, and have him consider the danger he may have put himself in, as well as the hurt he caused someone else by his actions, on the other.

MANAGING TEACHING DILEMMAS

In spite of her uncertainty and her conflicting feelings about what action to take, Ruth, in a quick moment, had to decide how to respond to Carlito and his work. She was both professionally and morally responsible for doing so. Functioning as such in the middle of uncertain choices is part of what it means to teach. Lampert (1985) suggests that rather than trying to "solve" these inevitable dilemmas of teaching, teachers must learn to manage them. This can begin with coming to recognize that teaching is fundamentally uncertain work in spite of the norm of certainty that seems to prevail in the profession currently. It is seldom easy for teachers to determine how to act when confronted with a situation that has a multitude of factors that need to be taken into account. And most situations in teaching fall into that category. Nor is there a guaranteed right answer for the "What should I do?" question. Instead the teacher is called upon to weigh the possible actions she might take and act according to what she believes is best for her students and any others involved.

The challenge, of course, is determining what "best" means in any given circumstance. Because teaching and learning happen in the context of human relationships, teachers must assess and respond to the needs, thoughts, emotions, and behaviors of others (typically their students). The complexity and uncertainty of those human factors require teachers to draw on different and often conflicting values, goals, and commitments as they determine how to act. The moral dimensions of teaching become clear as we recognize the complexity of the work and the role of the teacher in managing this uncertainty.

In Ruth's case the values pitted against one another were clear. She was committed to Carlito's academic progress and did not want to distract him. At the same time she felt a deep commitment to his social, emotional, and physical well-being. Either choice meant she was compromising some part of what she thought was in his best interest. Rather than solve the problem, Ruth had to manage it by choosing the action she believed would serve Carlito best. Watching his response guided her in taking the next step of their interaction.

The Dilemma Case Narratives

Ruth's narrative is one of a collection—a number of which are included in this book. She wrote it as part of a 5th-year teacher preparation course I teach entitled, Introduction to the Profession of Teaching Diverse Learners. I asked the novice teachers to write about an instance of practice, where they had to take an action but found it unclear as to what they should do. The narratives begin with a description of the context in which the incident took place and then a description of the incident itself, including as many details as possible, to give the reader a chance to experience it vicariously. The narratives include also a description of how the teacher reasoned through the dilemma considering both the purposes of her teaching and the consequences of any action she might take. If she resolved the dilemma, she included this as well. For many of the dilemma narratives discussed in the following pages there was no resolution at the time of the writing. Rather, the teachers presented their dilemma narratives to their colleagues in hopes that sharing them would help them decide what they should do. As you read about the teaching dilemmas included here, I encourage you to put yourself in the teacher's shoes and imagine what you would do if you found yourself facing the dilemma she or he describes.

CONSIDERING CONTEXT

Once one has accepted that teaching is uncertain work that will constantly challenge the teacher to make tough decisions driven by competing commitments, goals, and values, it might be useful to consider what types of circumstances are most likely to raise teaching dilemmas. McDonald (1992) describes the work of teaching as occurring in a "wild triangle of relations among teachers, students, and subjects . . . all of which shift continuously" (p. 1). In addition to the shifting nature of these relationships, another factor that makes the triangle of relations "wild" is the context within which it occurs. If the student, teacher, and subject are in a large city school we might expect the teachers' dilemmas to be different from those they would face were they teaching in a small school in a wealthy suburb or in a large school in a rural community. Whereas dilemmas occur in all teaching settings, a different context around a similar set of circumstances suggests a different framing of the teaching dilemma in each case and a different approach to managing it as well.

The urban context is a particularly uncertain and challenging one for teachers. On the one hand is the challenge of how to draw on the richness of the diverse community of families who live in urban centers and who have much to contribute to the school culture and environment. Creating boundary-spanning relationships with families and other community members, so that the school will reflect the desires, values, and needs of the community it serves, is important to the success of urban schools. On the other hand, balancing this goal with the goal of preparing students to learn the culture of power, which may not reflect the culture of the community, is challenging for novices and veterans alike (Delpit, 1995). The dilemma comes in wanting the students to be aware of and learn to function successfully in institutions reflecting the dominant culture, such as schools, while at the same time wanting them to not lose their other identities or feel that those identities are devalued. Urban schools are culturally rich, exciting places. How to make them work well for students is the challenge teachers face.

Along with the richness and vitality of any school setting are the unique challenges of that setting as well. This is true for all schools, urban schools included. Poverty, violence, and racism are compelling examples of societal factors that affect the of lives of many children in urban schools. Children who face those challenges typically struggle in school as they are distracted by the day-to-day circumstances of their lives outside of school (Orfield & Lee, 2005).

We might ask ourselves what are the challenges of the urban context that teachers might anticipate that raise dilemmas for them in their practice? How might we help novices and other teachers think about these challenges and their consequences before encountering them in their classrooms? We can begin by considering several characteristics of the urban setting that predictably raise dilemmas for teachers.

Poverty is one reality that impacts teachers' work in many urban schools. The poverty levels of students who go to urban schools typically parallel the poverty of the schools themselves. According to the 2010 report from in the State of America Children Yearbook, "The gap between the rich and the poor in the U.S. is the largest on record" (Children's Defense Fund). One in twelve children in the United States lives in extreme poverty with an income of less than $11,025 or lower per year for a family of four. They report also that African American and Hispanic children are more than twice as likely to be poor as White or non-Hispanic children. Research shows that poverty has a significant effect on school success, especially in settings where the school does not have adequate resources to address the special learning needs of poor children and, in particular, poor children of color (Berliner, 2009; Noguera, 2003). The schoolwork of children who arrive at school hungry or who don't have clothes warm enough for the rainy day raises many questions for teachers. Ida's dilemma provides an example.

Ida's Dilemma

Ida taught second grade in a small school that serves a poor neighborhood in a large west coast city. She explained that "the school's population is predominately African American (70%), Latino (18%), and the remaining 12% a mixture of Asian and Caucasian students." Her dilemma concerned Sharon, one of her students who never wore a coat or jacket to school even on the coldest of mornings and who was "frequently sick," possibly, because of this. As the fall days got colder, Ida loaned Sharon her own jacket so she'd have one for recess. Still, when Sharon left school at the end of the day, she did so without a coat or covering of any kind. Ida was concerned for Sharon's health. As a new teacher she was uncertain about what she should do. She decided to talk with the school principal who investigated the situation and learned that Sharon lost her jacket and her mother didn't have enough money to buy her a new one. At that point the school stepped in and bought her a jacket, which eased Ida's mind.

Having a jacket did not solve Sharon's problem of being cold, however, or Ida's problem of caring for her. She often forgot to wear her jacket and left it home or at school or somewhere in between. Ida described "one cloudy cold morning," in particular, when Sharon "came to school again without her jacket." "She was wearing her usual thin black stretch pants and her blue zip up shirt and nothing else," Ida explained. For the next several days Sharon arrived with no jacket even though the bad weather continued and even though she became sicker and sicker with a cold. Each day when Ida asked her where her jacket was Sharon repeatedly said simply that she didn't have it. Finally several days later after much prodding from Ida, Sharon claimed that her mother would not let her bring her jacket to school. Wondering if this were true, Ida decided to call Sharon's mom, who explained that Sharon was not allowed to bring her jacket as a form of discipline. Ida explained, she "decided to show her what it really feels like to be cold by not allowing her to bring her jacket to school as a way to punish her for not listening."

The layers of dilemmas this generated for Ida were many—whether or not to go along with the mother's wishes and let Sharon be in school without a coat, whether to try to talk with the mother about alternative disciplinary measures (which she did without success), whether to provide Sharon a jacket in the meantime. On the one hand, Ida felt responsible for Sharon's well-being. For Ida, having no coat and being cold at school was unacceptable. But she was not Sharon's mother and disregarding a mother's plan for disciplining her child did not seem like a good choice either. Again Ida was faced with the question of what she should do. She recognized that Sharon's mother had ultimate responsibility for Sharon. But she also felt responsible for Sharon's well-being. In deciding how to act, Ida struggled with how to deal with cultural differences, her own values as a teacher, her authority as a teacher, and her relationship with Sharon's mother. Ida's case provides an example of how poverty impacts school and raises many difficult dilemmas for teachers.

There are a number of other factors associated with poverty that heighten the uncertainties surrounding how best to meet students' academic needs. Research shows that poor children are more likely to struggle in school than their more affluent peers. According to the American Psychological Association's report (2011) on the effects of poverty, hunger, and homelessness on children and youth,

> Poorer children and teens are also at greater risk for several negative outcomes such as poor academic achievement, school dropout, abuse and neglect, behavioral and socioemotional problems, physical health problems, and developmental delays . . . The academic achievement gap for poorer youth is particularly pronounced for low-income African American and Hispanic children compared with their more affluent White peers.

Other characteristics of the urban setting predictably challenge teachers as well. Consider the lack of resources for example. Studies of school finance reveal large disparities in the allocation of resources, such as computers, books, supplies, physical facilities, and so on, between schools that serve affluent students and those that serve the urban poor, the majority of whom are children of color (Banks et al., 2005; Kozol, 1991). Providing a rigorous curriculum with high expectations and high standards for children when the system does not provide adequate resources raises serious dilemmas for teachers. Consider a teacher who has one set of books, which meets the reading level of a small minority of the class who need extra help in her diverse classroom but not of the majority of her students who are ready for more challenging literature. This teacher confronts a dilemma concerning both what and how to teach. Similarly, a teacher who does not have the subject-matter preparation to teach advanced algebra but is put into this position because there was "no one else to do it" faces the dilemma of whether to stay and try to teach something he really knows very little about or to leave the students with no teacher at all. He fears that the school will not replace him if he leaves, but to stay is a poor alternative given his lack of knowledge. In both cases the school does not have adequate resources to meet the students' needs and, yet, the teachers stand between this reality and serving their students well.

Violence, often a partner of poverty, is part of the daily lives of some children in large cities in the United States. It is another factor of the urban setting that impacts school life and raises challenging dilemmas for teachers. Children who are afraid and/or who have witnessed violent crimes against people they love are of necessity less present for the work of school than others who do not contend with such situations. But violence in the neighborhoods and outside of school is not the only problem; violence is becoming a bigger problem inside of school as well (Lee, 2007). Growing numbers of children are afraid to come to school, citing violence and gang activity in the hallways and school yards as their reason. Reports of bullying and sexual harassment in all schools, including urban schools, are also on the rise. Guns and other weapons add to the fear of violence felt in some schools and raise dilemmas about how to acknowledge the impact of violence on the students' lives, on the one hand, and not lower standards and thus compromise their educations, on the other.

Another factor that adds to the complexity of some urban school-children's lives and challenges teachers on how to act is immigration and the difficulty of becoming a legal citizen in the United States. Citizenship status puts a wedge between many immigrant parents and their children's schools. It is clear why parents who are labeled "illegal" are not likely to participate in school functions or report problems that their children are having in school. Fear keeps them away. The teacher who wants to connect with parents may do everything in her power to invite them into her classroom. She is eager for them to feel comfortable and welcome and, at the same time, she doesn't want to make them feel guilty if they cannot respond. She wonders how she can convince them that they would be safe in her classroom all the while realizing that in the eyes of many parents any contact with the school puts them in immediate danger of being deported. How to include parents and make them feel welcome and part of a school community involves building trust, which is challenging to do when the larger societal context within which schools exist threatens immigrant families.

With immigration come the issues of language, ethnicity, culture, and race, all of which raise dilemmas for teachers the majority of whom are White and monolingual. If they don't speak the language of their students, teachers worry that they are not serving them well. Those who are multilingual wonder what language they should speak with their students. Consider Emma.

Emma's Dilemma

Emma taught 5th grade in a large west coast city. The children in her class spoke a variety of languages at home, including English, Tagalog, and Spanish, which was Emma's first language. Two of the Spanish-speaking girls were recent Mexican immigrants who were delighted to learn that Emma had been born in Mexico. The two latched on to her immediately, consuming much of Emma's time and attention in spite of her determined attempts to attend to all children equally. Emma described her dilemma as concerning her relationships with these two students. It came to a head one day when she found herself explaining a difficult math concept to these two girls in Spanish, rather than English, the "official" (and shared) language of the classroom. She explained, "A few times I caught myself uttering something in Spanish rather than English, just because it was my first instinct when talking with these particular girls." Speaking in Spanish was so natural that she didn't become conscious of this, as she said, "until I glanced up and realized that one of the other students had heard me helping Silvia in Spanish and was looking at me in a confused way."

Emma wondered if "it [was] appropriate to use a child's native language in the classroom where there [were] other children who [did] not speak it." She described feeling torn because she would have liked to help students who were struggling with difficult content because they couldn't speak English. Explaining things in their language would certainly help— she knew this from her own experience as a second language learner new to U.S. schools. To not speak in Spanish when she knew it would facilitate the girls' learning felt to Emma like she was not doing all she could do to help them. At the same time, she explained, "I know that when a language other than English is being spoken it can often come with a feeling of exclusivity on behalf of those who may not speak it." Additionally, she wondered if speaking Spanish would give some students an advantage over others. She worried, too, about whether helping in Spanish might be at the price of helping the students become more fluent in English, the language of school.

Emma's case and others like it point to the importance of culture and cultural differences that are so prevalent in urban school settings. Research tells us how culture impacts learning and how important it is for teachers to recognize the importance of drawing on the students' cultures and prior experiences as we prepare to teach them well

(Gonzáles, Moll, & Amanti, 2005; Lee, 2007; Ladson-Billings, 1994, 2001). Through the narrative cases we can see how the richness that comes with a diverse classroom of students simultaneously raises complicated dilemmas for the teachers.

LAYERS OF COMPLEXITY IN MANAGING CONTEXT-BASED DILEMMAS

Though we have focused on the more problematic circumstances of the urban setting because our interest here is in considering how the school context raises predictable dilemmas for teachers, it is important for us to keep in mind that not all of the dilemmas of teaching caused by the complexity of the urban context are negative. Emma's dilemma that describes how a shared culture between the students and their teacher provided for a bond that formed the student-teacher relationship is an example. The complexity of the urban context, which presents multiple opportunities for learning about people different from oneself and sharing those differences, can be extremely positive. However, even when positive this complication can raise challenging circumstances that stump even the most experienced teacher. Consider the joy of being part of a large extended family and community that is part of the life experience of many children of immigrant parents. These familial connections are often the envy of the students whose families are small and isolated.

While the large extended family is an asset for many children who have different adults and siblings to turn to for guidance and help, teaching dilemmas crop up from this positive example as well. Large families have greater needs for food, housing, and the like, and someone in the family needs to provide for them. Parents and older siblings work to provide the money the family needs, which sometimes puts younger children in charge of caring for even younger siblings. School attendance can be erratic when this occurs. At the same time these children are learning to care for others, taking responsibility for their families, and carrying out the traditions of their culture. How to honor those qualities and still insist on good attendance is a teaching dilemma.

Race, language, and culture are also all factors of the lively context of urban schools. For many teachers it is those characteristics that attract them to working in this setting in the first place. Teaching a diverse population of students who represent various cultures, beliefs, languages and ways of being in the world makes teaching exciting. But along with that excitement comes a good amount of uncertainty that challenges teachers—especially new teachers—as they strive for equity and social justice in their classrooms and schools. Culturally different ways of interacting with authority, of being with peers, of sharing space, and of learning are all steeped in traditions that present dilemmas for teachers who want to support the learning and academic success of all students.

The teacher narratives included in this book explore how the uncertain nature of teaching raises dilemmas for teachers that cannot be solved but must be managed instead. We will consider dilemmas faced by teachers teaching and learning to teach in urban schools and think through how this particular context—as is true for every different school context—raises a particular set of dilemmas for which teachers can prepare. The conception of teaching on which the book rests is one that acknowledges both the uncertain nature of teaching and the agency of teachers as decision makers in that uncertain context. As the field moves towards increasing standardization, which is guided by a myth of certainty, it is important to consider alternative views of the work and prepare teachers for what history and experience tell us they will encounter in their day-to-day practice.

CONCLUDING THOUGHTS

Schools are complex, changing places characterized as much by uncertainty as by anything else; there are but a handful of things the teacher can count on with certainty. One of those is that she will face countless dilemmas daily—situations that require her to act while knowing that what is in the best interest of her students is not at all clear. Learning to tolerate that ambiguity and manage those dilemmas are critical components of learning to teach. In this chapter we have posed the challenge of managing dilemmas and have begun to consider how teachers might go about accomplishing this aspect of their complex work.

A place to begin the work of managing teaching dilemmas is to learn to distinguish between problems of practice that can be reasoned through and solved and dilemmas of practice that defy direct resolution. Take, for example, a math teacher who wants to have her students demonstrate their mathematical thinking by showing their solutions to their homework problems on the classroom's whiteboards. She realizes quickly when the school year begins that her room does not have adequate whiteboard space to make this possible. She can solve this problem by ordering more whiteboards.

That same math teacher faces a dilemma rather than a problem when she considers how to assess her students in her heterogeneous beginning algebra class. The majority of her group seems to be making good progress as the year gets under way, but there is another group who arrived without adequate background to be successful in the class. At the time of her first unit test she had the idea that instead of constructing a test geared at the middle level between these two groups, she might create two tests so that those who were making good progress would be challenged and those at the lower level would have a chance at success and not be discouraged as the new year begins. But she wonders if that is a good solution. She does not want to lose her lower-level students by having them take a test that she (and they) knew they would likely fail. At the same time she wants to have high expectations for all her students and fears two-tiered test might suggest that she is holding lower expectations for some.

This teacher is on the horns of a dilemma. To manage it, as we will see happening for the dilemmas considered in the following chapters of this book, this teacher must consider both her purpose (or purposes) for administering the test in the first place and the consequences of either action for both groups of students. Her challenge comes in realizing that she could argue for both approaches to the test question—create two separate tests or stick with one test for the full group. Yet she has to make a choice—and quickly as the test date is less than a week away. As difficult as it is to make a decision, ultimately she must do so. Her work involves reasoning the dilemma through to the best of her ability, making a decision, and then acting. Confronting dilemmas like this is hard work.

In the chapters that follow I argue that as uncertain as the world of schools is, there is predictability to the kinds of dilemmas teachers face, which can make the process of managing dilemmas a little easier. This predictability, which is attached to understanding one's teaching context, is another factor that can help teachers manage the dilemmas that confront them daily. Teaching is context bound. Understanding the context of the school where one teaches can help teachers anticipate what factors might raise dilemmas for them. We considered in this chapter a variety of contextual factors in the urban setting—race, class, and language differences, for example—that raise predictable dilemmas for teachers.

In reviewing more than 300 dilemma cases for this book, I found there were four areas of teaching concern into which many of the cases fell: (1) forming a professional identity, (2) building strong student-teacher relationships, (3) constructing a relevant curriculum, and (4) assessing students in meaningful and productive ways. Whereas these four areas were consistent throughout all the cases, it was notable how the different contexts in which teachers were working revealed important dilemma differences with regard to each area of concern. A teacher forming a professional identity teaching in a high-income community, for example, might find herself wondering if she "measures up" to the parents' expectations of who their child's teacher should be. An identity dilemma for a teacher in an urban school might focus on her own judgment about her competence and professional identity as a teacher when she does not speak the same language as her students and their parents.

This book focuses on teaching in the urban setting and the ways this context raises dilemmas for teachers. My hope is that by studying the dilemmas of the teacher-authors in each of the areas of concern (identity, student-teacher relationships, curriculum, and assessment), the reader will develop an understanding of how the context of one's teaching suggests a set of predictable dilemmas—and that this predictability will shape the teacher's ability to manage these dilemmas in the future.

CHAPTER 2

Who Am I as Teacher?

Dilemmas of Professional Identity Development

> As an instructor in this program I continually re-evaluate my role and responsibilities. I notice a dramatic gap between the goals I set for myself, and my actual ability to inspire and motivate students. Now, when I reflect on my role in the classroom, I see myself as a coach at best, and mostly a babysitter, a common enemy, a nag, a caricature, erratic, neurotic, idealistic, and desperately underprepared. I am an imposter, a young observer of the world walking stiffly in a newly purchased teacher wardrobe that I cannot wait to shed, with nothing in my bookbag but persisting hope and the best of intentions.
>
> Lucy, *"An Imposter?"*

Lucy wonders how she'll ever become a "real" teacher—the kind she envisioned she'd be when she started out on this professional path. She wonders when she will know enough and be able to make good decisions fast enough to serve her students well. Her preparation and her new teacher clothes fall far short of giving her the confidence she needs to grapple with her many questions about "what she should do" as she faces each new teaching challenge. The comment above reflects her struggle as a novice to assume authority even when the school rules are clear and what needs to be done is fairly clear as well. But for Lucy and many other new teachers like her, knowing what steps to take in any particular situation is seldom clear.

The incident that motivated Lucy's comment occurred one day when she witnessed a student showing his classmates a pocketknife he had brought to school. At the time she was teaching middle school in a large urban district. She knew she had to take immediate action, but she was unsure what that action should be. Previously she had noticed how this particular boy was left out when the students hung around together, which made her reluctant to single him out in front of his friends. Plus she wondered if singling him out could provoke an angry and perhaps dangerous response. At the same time, he had broken an important school rule and he and the other students needed to know this in no uncertain terms.

Even in a case like this where the school rules are unambiguous, knowing how or why to act can be difficult for teachers. For the novice it is more difficult still especially if her prior school and life experiences were different from those of her students. Bullying was part of Lucy's middle school life, but responding with a weapon was not. She knew she needed to take the boy's knife and make the school rules clear to both the student and his friends. But in the moment all she could think was, "What should I do?"

In spite of her internal struggle, Lucy acted quickly, demanding that the student give her his knife. He gave it to her without incident but "implored" her to give it back to him after school. In their conversation at the end of the day she asked why he brought the knife in the first place knowing it was against school rules. His frank response disarmed her: "Because some kids told me they were going to jump me after school and I needed to protect myself." Alarmed by the danger the student felt and moved by his pleading, Lucy considered if she should return the knife. She worried for his safety and wondered if having his knife with him would actually make him safe. Maybe he would be less safe having the knife. She also wondered about her role and if she was responsible for the student once he left the school grounds. In the end, she acquiesced, returned the knife and "instructed him to go straight home." Moments later another student who witnessed the exchange asked in disbelief, "You gave it back to him? Are you *trying* to get somebody killed?"

In that moment Lucy realized what she had done. Fear flooded her. As a teacher, she knew she was responsible for not only this child's safety but for the safety of the other children in his class and in his community. She agonized over the danger she put others in by her decision. "What should I have done?" she asked herself repeatedly. Whereas the school rules are clear about no weapons on campus, in that moment of decision making, she simply lost track of those rules. Instead, she responded to her student's pleading; he felt he was in danger and having his knife would protect him.

"I wondered about a long cut on his forehead and I experienced intense panic," she wrote. "With only my student's safety in mind, I acted in the best way I could think to do at the time. Did I make a mistake?"

Lucy's concerns about this particular decision and its consequences—real and potential—were tethered to her concerns about her role and identity as a teacher as well as her knowledge of communities very different from her own. Day after day she found herself reflecting on how uncertain she felt in her new role, especially as she realized often how much the decisions she made as a teacher mattered in her students' lives. Her lack of familiarity with the setting combined with the seriousness of the responsibility to do right by her students left her unsettled at the close of school each day. She felt like an imposter. As for her decision to return the knife, she wondered if it "compromised (her) authority as a responsible adult." Did she "put [herself] at risk" for having "exposed her decision making to her students"? Lucy acted in a way she thought was right at the moment, but thinking about it further, she realized how wrong it might have been.

BECOMING A TEACHER

Knowing how to act in the role of teacher is an acquired capability that builds over a lifetime. As we reflect on the decisions we make to see if they align with what we learn the role requires and what we believe, our sense of self in this important work becomes clearer. Developing a professional identity and acting from that place of knowing oneself is an important and yet challenging part of teaching especially as one begins to realize how significant the teacher is and can be in her students' lives.

For novices, the journey is particularly challenging. As we saw with Lucy, novice teachers "are expected to act the part before they fully grasp or identify with new roles" (Ronfeldt & Grossman, 2008, p. 42). The point at which the new teacher realizes how much she has to learn, not only about how to teach, but about the context in which that teaching will occur, produces tension for most novice teachers who are learning to stand with confidence on the teacher's side of the desk. Out of this tension arise dilemmas when teachers' "different identities suggest contradictory solution paths" to the questions they confront in their practice day to day (Enyedy, Goldberg, & Muir, 2005, p. 72). Like what we witnessed with Lucy, who struggled to reconcile her need to respond to her student's perceived need for safety and her important role in keeping her students safe, the novice teacher narratives provide abundant examples of these existential and ethical dilemmas.

PROFESSIONAL IDENTITY AND
THE URBAN SCHOOL CONTEXT

Professional identity in teaching is constructed in a context that has historical and structural meanings as well as cultural practices, all of which influence the teacher's understanding of herself in that role (Beijaard, Meijer, & Verloop, 2004). Many who write about teacher identity refer to the work of Herbert Mead (1964), who studied meaning making in human beings. Mead explained that human beings act in response to things that have meaning for them. For teachers in particular, those meanings develop over the many years they spend in school, beginning with their lives as students before they even enter their formal professional preparation (Holland, Lachicotte, Skinner, & Cain, 2001; Lortie, 1975). During their extended time in schools, teachers' conceptions develop about what it means to teach and what teachers do. Many teachers, including those highlighted in this book, attended schools and developed these conceptions in settings different from those in which they have chosen to teach. The result is predictable confusion as they try to interpret the messages given by their new school context, with its realities, rules, regulations, and rituals about what the role entails. Incorporating the revised role with prior conceptions of who one is and wants to be as a teacher is challenging indeed.

What are the characteristics of the urban context that are difficult for new teachers to manage? As we saw in Lucy's case and also in Ruth's, which we considered in Chapter 1, violence is one especially for teachers who have had little experience with acts of violence themselves. Violence is often connected with poverty, which is another reality of many urban settings and a challenge for teachers who come from middle-class homes. Children bring with them to school expressions of their lives outside of school. Part of learning to teach in urban schools and developing an identity as a teacher in this setting involves coming to better understand the context that frames the lives of the students and the students' families.

Another characteristic of many urban schools that we have not yet considered is the high level of externally imposed standardization and

regulation. The urban setting has many schools that are underperform-
ing as measured by the standardized tests associated with the No Child
Left Behind (NCLB) legislation. In response, NCLB mandates program
structures aimed at raising academic performance, such as curricula that
tell teachers what to teach, pacing guides that tell teachers how long
to spend on any given topic, and regular standardized testing designed
to measure student success. The idea of these strategies is that by standardizing the learning opportunities afforded children we can level the
playing field so that all children will have equal opportunities to learn
and achieve academically. The challenge, of course, comes in recognizing that the children one teaches are far from "standard," especially in
urban schools where diversity, in terms of race, class, culture, and language, is the norm.

Teachers who are monitored under such mandates become conflicted
about their role and their identity as teachers, especially when they enter
a profession that they believe requires independence, judgment, and personal responsibility. Olsen (2008), who studied the relationship between
the reasons people choose to become teachers and their experience of
the work, found that "many first year teachers experience fundamental
identity conflicts as they work to reconcile long-held expectations with
current teaching realities" (p. 37). As we see in this next example from
Laura, one of those external mandates that predictably raises a teaching
dilemma is the standardized test.

Laura's Dilemma

Laura taught fourth grade in an urban elementary school. Of her
27 students "eighteen [were] Latino, three [were] African American,
three [were] Caucasian, and three [were] Asian. Fifteen of the Latino
students [were] bilingual and most [were] biliterate." One of Laura's students, Rosa, for whom the year was her first in a U.S. school, was neither
bilingual nor biliterate.

Laura's dilemma began to take shape on the day of the Stanford
Achievement Test, Ninth Edition (SAT9) writing sample, which was
at that time a district-required test that all students had to take regard-
less of their language proficiency in English.[1] The test asked students to
read a page-long text about frogs and toads and then write a summary of
what they read. Laura explained that although the content of the text was
not above Rosa's listening comprehension capability (although perhaps

outside of her life experience) it was beyond her reading level in English. Laura's partner teacher who had administered this test many times before, explained to Laura that whereas there would be students who did not understand the text of the test—Rosa and her classmate Jorge being at the head of this list—the teachers were not allowed to provide any help in addition to the directions they read (in English) at the outset of the test administration. She then shared the same information with the students:

> In giving the instructions, my partner teacher explained that some students who are learning English may not be able to understand very much from the text or write very much and that they should just try to recognize and write the words they do know.

It was no surprise that Rosa was lost from the moment the test began. Not only did she not understand the text she was to read, she did not understand what she was to write on the lined paper that was placed under the test booklet in front of her. When she saw her classmates reading and writing, Rosa raised her hand to ask what she was supposed to do. Laura reported,

> I said I was sorry, but I couldn't translate the instructions for her or help her with the writing. I wanted to tell Rosa to just ignore the test and read her book. It felt very uncomfortable as a teacher to tell a student, "I can't help you," and it felt completely pointless for this child to take this assessment. I wondered what we were communicating to Rosa and Jorge by requiring them to take an exam which was far beyond their English abilities and so different from their work in the classroom.

Laura's message to "read her book" did not settle well with Rosa who saw the children around her still writing on their papers. She began copying verbatim the frog article the students had been asked to read maybe thinking that she, too, should be writing and not knowing what else to write. When Laura walked by Rosa's desk a few minutes later she saw that "she had copied over a paragraph into the answer booklet." Rosa turned to Laura once again and asked "if she should write more." Laura responded:

> I said if she felt done, she could stop and read her book. She kept staring at the exam and copying, perhaps because all the other

students were still working. A couple of minutes passed and I walked by her again; she asked me what she should do. I told her she seemed done and should read her book.

Laura struggled with figuring out what to do to help Rosa, but also with figuring out her role as a teacher and her role as an agent of the state that requires tests that make no sense. The school and testing rules mandated her to act in a way that conflicted with what she believed was in her students' best interest. Asking a child to take a test in English when she doesn't read or write English and then not help her understand what was happening and why was far from Laura's conception of professional, ethical behavior. If she were to act as she believed teachers should act in seeing a student as lost as Rosa was, she would help her interpret the directions of the test and guide her toward a solution that would lessen her anxiety. As it was, she was being asked to act in a way that conflicted with what she viewed as central to her emerging professional identity. And she was troubled to find herself acting in accordance with those expectations.

From the outset Laura knew that it made no sense to administer the SAT9 to Rosa and her classmate Jorge. She wrote:

This assessment was disconnected from the instruction they are receiving and from their current English literacy skills. It will not provide any new or useful information. The assessment is not aligned with the teachers' goals for these children, nor with any reasonable goals for them. In addition, this seems like an invalidating and miseducative experience for both children.

It was uncomfortable for Laura and painful to have to force Rosa to sit through the test without guidance. And yet as a teacher in the school where the test was mandated, she felt she had to comply with the requirements of her job. Comforting her student would have aligned with what she envisioned to be her role as Rosa's teacher; withholding information was not. Laura continued to wonder what she should do and what kind of response she should have when her beliefs and her sense of what she ought to do as the person responsible for "doing no harm" so clearly conflicted with what appeared to be required of the job. She wondered if pursuing this further with her partner teacher and others at her site would make sense, or if in her position as a new teacher she should, in this instance, go along with what the testing rules required.

Laura and Lucy struggled to negotiate the terrain between themselves and the context in which they do their work. For Laura it was the context's mandate for standardized tests, on the one hand, and the student population of recent immigrant children who didn't yet speak English on the other, that caused her dilemma. For Lucy it was the contextual factor of violence in the community where she taught caused her to question whether she should return the student's knife to him so he would feel safe walking home from school or hold onto his knife, realizing that the knife would probably make him less rather than more safe for his journey. Both teachers wondered not only about what to do but what their role as teacher required them to do. Adding to their confusion was their sense that they had to take action that did not align with what they believed in or were familiar with from their past.

Most schools provide little time or opportunity for teachers to step back and ask, "What am I doing?" and "Why?" If professional identity arises—at least in part—out of the teachers' interactions with "the socially constructed roles, meaning systems, and symbols of the cultural context they encounter" (Horn, Nolen, Ward, & Campbell, 2008, p. 62), we can begin to see why it is important to consider the ways in which the urban context both shapes and challenges the development of the teacher's professional identity. Recognizing the impact of context, we can anticipate the tension that will arise when a teacher finds her way into a new and unfamiliar environment and prepares for managing the dilemmas that will predictably occur.

RACE AND LANGUAGE IN THE URBAN SCHOOL CONTEXT

Many teachers who teach in urban schools choose to do so because of the culturally rich environment the urban setting provides. Racial, cultural, ethnic, language, and class differences among students and teachers—all features of the urban setting—bring a vitality that has the potential to energize the work. At the same time, urban schools are often subject to social and political forces that structure and institutionalize inequities that challenge schools and teachers to be able to actualize the potential of that richness. Diversity means difference. Racial and ethnic differences open many doors and potentially many new opportunities for teachers and students. However, in many schools racism often negates that potential. In school, like in society in general, not all differences are equally valued.

In fact, some differences are systematically devalued—for example, skin color, language, and cultural ways of knowing. Whereas there is always considerable diversity in how children react to school, most children who are White, English speaking, and middle class have a good chance of fitting in. They are used to the rules that schools put forth. They speak the language of the teacher and of the texts they will be required to read. They recognize the systems that order the school day. This feeling of comfort with how things are may be missing in children whose language and culture are different from that of their White, middle-class peers.

Most discussions of the urban school equate the context with large metropolitan settings characterized by linguistically, racially, and culturally diverse populations of students (Hammerness & Matsko, 2010). These communities have disproportionately higher rates of families in poverty and schools that are under-resourced (Kozol, 1991; Oakes & Lipton, 2003). As argued earlier, associated with poverty is violence, another factor challenging teaching and learning in urban schools (Noguera, 1995, 2003). Developing a teacher identity in this context involves finding a way of grappling with the particular complexities of the setting while holding onto one's choice to teach in the first place. It also involves coming to better understand one's own racial and class identity and how these identity factors impact one's work.

Many teachers who teach in urban schools are driven by a desire to open new learning opportunities for children who have not thus far been served well by their schools. Their identities as teachers are closely tied to the particular work they are hoping to do in this setting. For many teachers of color, their professional identity is often closely tied to their racial identity and to their strong commitment to teach with the goals of equity and social justice. Encountering the effects of racism on the students they serve renders professional-identity development especially challenging. Consider Elsie.

Elsie's Dilemma

Elsie is an African American teacher of English in a middle school that she described as "a school of color, with less than seven percent of students identifying as White." She described her students as bringing "incredible cultural legacies into the classroom" and being "definitely aware of race and culture." As a middle school teacher she was particularly aware of this being a time of identity formation in the students' lives.

"Developmentally speaking," she wrote, "this is the time when students begin exploring and forming their racial and cultural identities." It was also the time when Elsie embarked on her own identity journey—exploring what it meant to be a teacher and figuring out where her identity as an African American female fit in. Elsie's dilemma occurred when she was challenged by her students to conform to an understanding of Blackness different from her own. Managing that dilemma influenced her growing understanding of what it means to be a Black teacher in a school that serves a high percentage of children of color. She wrote:

> All of my students want to know more about me (how old I am, my first name). However, my Black students do not want just answers. That is, they are constantly in the process of assessing me. From my mannerisms, the way I speak and dress, to the music I play in class, they are comparing me to their definition of Blackness.

While Elsie was trying to figure out the role of her own Blackness in her professional identity, her students were at the same time analyzing who she was and who they were with regard to race. "Based on this analysis," she worried they would decide "not only whether they [liked] me, but how they [would] treat me, and how they [would] behave in the classroom."

Elsie's dilemma surfaced one day, soon after she had started teaching at the school. She had planned what she thought of as a "fairly routine activity" that had students rotating around through five stations and answering different reading comprehension questions at each. Her role was to "float around from station to station answering clarifying questions and cajoling students to complete the work." At the second of these five stations, the question asked students "if and when it is appropriate to lie." The students were talking this through when Elsie approached, and Damion, one of the Black students in the group, asked Elsie if she smoked weed. "It was obvious that he and several other students expected the answer to be yes," she wrote. And when she provided the honest answer no, she felt that the students assumed she was not telling the truth. Her attempt to convince them otherwise was to no avail.

Elsie began to see what she was up against as she envisioned her struggle against racism in her new role as teacher. Though she realized she was confronting a class difference between herself and her students, she was nonetheless frustrated by their response, which she interpreted as an example of debilitating internalized oppression. Her students held a view of

Blackness as a culture associated with drugs. Being Black to them meant "doing drugs"; not doing drugs called into question how Black one can be.

Elsie was not surprised by her students' view. These were teenagers after all, probably living in a community where drugs were commonplace and where, at least in their developing views of the world, doing drugs indicated a modicum of belonging. Her motivation for being a teacher was driven by a desire to stop ideas like this from becoming the view students had about life in urban settings and what it meant to be Black. She felt an immediate call to action but was unsure where and how to start: What steps should she take to interrupt what she saw as the perpetuation of racial stereotypes in her classroom and expand her students' understanding of Black identity?

Elsie framed her dilemma as having two parts. The first concerned boundaries. She wondered how much teachers should tell students about their personal lives and, consequently, how much she should reveal about her own life to her students. "How much personal information is too much?" she asked. She wondered, too, if she should have ducked out of answering Damion's question about smoking weed. She realized that by responding she may have unintentionally invited him into a space where he felt privileged to ask her more. At the same time, she felt that answering Damion's question honestly allowed her a chance to see how race gets played out in classrooms, and how important it was to challenge what she called a "predictable cultural script"—one that begins with, "Act One: Smoking Weed."

As a Black teacher who had chosen to teach in a setting where most students were students of color, Elsie wrote that she wanted to become a role model—a Black woman who had experienced success in school and had not compromised her Black identity in doing so. But she wondered how much of this role-model stance involved revealing things about herself. To be a role model for her Black students, she knew she needed to earn their trust. But how? Figuring out how much her students needed to know about her as a person outside of school was one aspect of her dilemma. She explained that, compared to her second concern, "this question [was] fairly easy to tease out."

Elsie found managing the second part of her dilemma much more difficult. It concerned her role in challenging her students' conceptions of race and of what "being Black" could mean. "How do I push back on students' narrow-minded/stereotypical definition of Blackness, not tell them how to think, but encourage them to think and question, without damaging their self concept?" she asked. Reflecting on her students' conceptions of Blackness and the role of class in framing that conception, she grappled with wanting to support them to develop healthy racial identities. Simultaneously, she grappled with understanding how her own racial identity fit into who she was and wanted to be as a teacher. Being Black was centrally important to her identity as a person and also how she saw herself in her new role as teacher. But she wanted the understanding of her Black identity to reflect who she was and not who her students thought she was because of their stereotypic conceptions. Because part of that identity development for teachers comes from their students' regard for them in this role, Elsie's students' misunderstanding of her racial identity rendered the identity process especially complicated.

Elsie pondered the consequence of their view of Black identity for her teaching and her students' learning. She wrote,

> Because I am Black my Black students have ideas about how I should
> be. When my words and actions do not match their ideas they
> reject me as "real." This creates a problem with students believing
> that I understand what they are going through inside and outside
> of school. This disconnect hinders my ability to reach students, to
> create meaningful relationships and experiences that lead to an
> increased knowledge of self and the world at large, and a drive to
> take action against oppressive forces.

There is a painful irony here for Elsie who entered teaching with the goal of working with Black students, to help them better understand how racism functions in the "world at large" so that they could "take action against oppressive forces" and ultimately open new opportunities for themselves and their communities. Her purpose was clear, as was her dilemma. What was not clear was what she should do. She believed that because her life did not conform to what her students had "observed as typical Black amongst Black people in their community and in the media" she feared she had become "an outsider" to them—someone in their eyes "not really Black." The class difference between Elsie and her students accentuated her dilemma. While conceding, "This status as an outsider is both hurtful and discouraging," Elsie knew she had to hold onto her racial identity as she developed herself as a teacher committed to making a difference in her students' lives. She wrote: "What I have to do is construct lessons that allow students to see the dangers in binaries, to understand that Blackness lives on an ever expanding spectrum." The work is both "deeply personal and political," she said, but "authentic teaching and learning [would] not take place until students and myself take it on."

Related to race and ethnicity, language is another aspect of the urban context that raises questions of identity for teachers. Most urban schools serve high percentages of students whose home languages are other than English. Additionally, many children who speak English as their home language speak a dialect of English different from the English spoken at school. Since the experience of school for both students and teachers is mediated through language (Lee, 2007; Moll, 2000; Vygotsky, 1978), we can begin to see the many ways language differences impact teachers and raise dilemmas concerning their teaching roles and identities. We saw in the case of Emma in Chapter 1 how sharing a common home language with a subset of students raised a challenging dilemma for her. In her role as the teacher for a class of students only a third of whom shared Spanish with her as their first language, Emma wondered if using Spanish in her classroom was appropriate. She questioned how much of her personal identity as a Latina she should bring into her role as teacher. The role seemed to raise a tension for her between what came naturally in speaking with her Spanish-speaking students and what she reasoned was required in her role as a teacher in a multicultural/multilingual classroom.

Sophie, whose dilemma we will consider next, provides another example of how the contextual factor of language can raise an identity dilemma for a novice teacher. Sophie ends her narrative wondering if she "has what it takes" to fulfill the role of bilingual teacher. We can follow her dilemma narrative and see how she arrived at that point.

Sophie's Dilemma

Sophie teaches third grade in an urban elementary school. She approached her new teaching assignment with great enthusiasm. She felt well prepared for this and looked forward to the work ahead. The context in which Sophie taught was 100% Spanish speaking. Of her students she wrote, "All are Latinos, and all are of Mexican descent . . . many of them were born in Mexico and began their schooling there." She noted that her partner teacher was an African American woman who spoke Spanish as her second language.

As a White teacher preparing to teach in this setting, Sophie knew that the role required her to have a good command of Spanish. She was a competent Spanish speaker and could converse with ease, but she was still determined to improve her proficiency. To do so she took a heavy academic load during her 2-year program of professional preparation, enrolling in Spanish classes along with her teacher education classes. Additionally she spent the intervening summers in Mexico where she could learn not only the language, but also the culture of her future students. By the time Sophie stepped into her first classroom she was ready. She felt clear about her identity as a White woman committed to issues of equity who chose to live out that commitment by teaching in a Spanish bilingual classroom. She had made good progress on meshing her personal identity with her emerging professional one.

But the teaching context presented challenges that caused Sophie to question whether or not she had "what it takes" to be the bilingual teacher she wanted to be. Her dilemma came to a head one day during a math lesson. The children were playing a fractions game called Cover-Up when Ernesto came to the front to take his turn rolling the dice. In order to "finish covering the whole," Sophie explained, "We needed the next person to roll a four, or the next two people to roll eights." Knowing this, "Ernesto turned the die around and around in his hands before strategically releasing it." When it came up a four, the children started cheering. It took a minute or two before Sophie realized that in midst of this cheering crowd one boy began chanting "*Chiteo, Chiteo, Chiteo*" and that quickly the others joined in, "chanting along their arms raised in the air." Before she knew it all had joined in the fun. It took a minute or two for Sophie to catch up with the excitement because it had erupted so quickly. She did not know what *chiteo* meant, but she knew that she had to calm the group before she could find out.

Sophie's sense of herself as a competent bilingual teacher was challenged by her not knowing what the word meant that was fueling such enthusiasm in her students. She wanted to respond appropriately to the class outbreak, but was at a loss as to how, given she did not know what they were saying. At the same time she was concerned about Ernesto who stood quietly facing his chanting classmates. Seeing herself as a caring teacher concerned with the emotional and physical safety in her room, she wanted to address his needs if, in fact, his classmates were turning against him as it appeared they were. Her thoughts also went back to her role as a teacher in a bilingual classroom. Knowing she had responsibility for helping students develop second language learning skills, she saw happenings like this wherein she did not know the word and needed help in learning it as an opportunity to model for the children about learning new words in a language when one does not know them. She wondered what she should do—and what she should do first.

Sophie decided that before she could do anything else she had to find out what *chiteo* meant so she could address the situation. She turned to Ernesto to see how he was doing and then she moved quickly to address the other responsibilities her role required. She explained,

> Ernesto was smiling. He sat down at his desk as I stopped and quieted the class in order to ask them what they were chanting. I often find myself asking questions and being explicit with the kids about what I don't yet know about Spanish hoping to set a positive model for them about second language learning strategies. With the children's help I figured out that *chiteo* means cheater.

Upon learning that the students were chanting "cheater," Sophie was quick to speak up on Ernesto's behalf. She explained that he was not a cheater; he was lucky. She reported also that she saw him roll the die just as his classmates had done before him.

Sophie hoped her strong statement and serious demeanor would help dismiss the charge and set the class back on track. However, she quickly realized that doing so was not so easy or straightforward a task. The students were riled up and, though Ernesto continued to smile, she sensed that he was sad. She was unclear what to do next. Should she turn her attention to Ernesto, which would satisfy her goal of being a caring teacher who attended to her students' feelings as they arise? Or should she take his smile as an indicator that he accepted her dismissal of the students' claim and move on to the curricular agenda she had planned for the day? She didn't want to put Ernesto into a position of more distress by belaboring the incident, but she didn't want to abandon him either. Plus, she wanted to get on with the mathematics lesson, which had been moving along well before all this had occurred. In this way she would fulfill her role as a teacher committed to holding high standards for her students' academic work.

A few minutes passed as the class continued on with the next step of her lesson plan, writing number sentences on the board with the children. Sophie looked over at Ernesto and noticed that he "had put his head down on his arms with his face hidden from view." Martin, Ernesto's friend, told Sophie that Ernesto was crying. Ernesto either "couldn't or wouldn't" tell her why he was upset. "He would only nod or shake his head in response to my questions," she wrote. His classmates offered various hypotheses: "One girl thought it had to do with him being excluded at recess. Others thought it had to do with the chanting." It wasn't until later when Sophie's partner teacher came in and Sophie was able to ask her to talk with Ernesto, that she learned that he was crying because his friends called him a cheater.

Sophie responded immediately. She called the group together to choose ways to apologize. Several came up with ideas, and in the end they decided a full-class apology was in order. When Ernesto returned to the classroom after his conversation with Sophie's partner teacher, Sophie invited him to the circle "where he stood next to me as the class apologized." "His face lit up in a smile," she reported with relief. When she checked in with Ernesto later in the day, "He said he felt good." Though this made Sophie feel better, it didn't stop her from wondering about her identity as a bilingual teacher. Not knowing the language well enough to respond quickly to help Ernesto and the others who were concerned about him caused her to question her identity and her suitability for the role she had chosen for herself. She wrote, "I wonder if my students deserve better than what I can give."

Sophie was clear that language—her own and that of her students—was at the core of her ability to fulfill her various roles as teacher. Though ultimately she felt she was able to handle the immediate dilemma of caring for Ernesto, the overarching dilemma of her identity as a caring bilingual teacher continued to grip her. She explained:

> I suppose you could say that the moment that I have described in the classroom was a culmination and a combination of my doubts and fears about my role as a bilingual teacher. My desire to teach in a bilingual classroom sometimes feels at odds with what I believe is best for my students. From time to time I feel very frustrated that I cannot do what I know to do, what I am able to do when speaking English, my first language. While I feel good about my choice to address the situation with Ernesto, and while I feel I did the best I could, my dilemma is not knowing if my best is good enough for my students. Is it fair to my students or to myself for me to be simultaneously learning a second language and learning to teach, while learning to teach in that language?

Sophie and Emma both struggled with their teacher identities and what was required of them given the language demands of the context in which they were teaching. Their uncertainty revolved around both the language needs of their students and their own personal language identity. Sophie worried that she did not know enough Spanish to be a bilingual teacher—an identity she had been working hard to assume. Emma, on the other hand, was bilingual and struggled with how her personal identity as a Latina, including the knowledge and capability that came with it, intersected with her role as a teacher.

Sophie and Emma are not alone when it comes to constructing a professional identity in the context of the complex and changing urban school. We learn from other teachers who have struggled with similar challenges that identity dilemmas arising from the language demands of teaching in multilingual classrooms are not uncommon. Ballenger (1992), for example, published a compelling narrative about her struggle to feel competent in her role as a teacher of Haitian children. It took learning from her Haitian teaching colleagues how to communicate effectively with them before she could assume authority effectively in her classroom. Her professional identity and her sense of herself as a competent teacher were challenged before learning these essential communication patterns. Similarly, Delpit (1995) had to learn the ways of the Native American people with whom she worked in Alaska before she saw herself as a competent teacher in that setting. In her essay "Hello Grandfather," she illustrates how learning the language of her students involves learning not only the words of their language but the customs and beliefs expressed by that language as well.

From these examples we can see how the multiplicity of languages spoken in urban schools that serve high populations of African, Asian, Native American, Latino, and other immigrant students challenge teachers who are constructing and reconstructing their professional identities. "Who am I to teach children whose first language and culture are ones that I am just learning?"—for example, "What is the appropriate language of authority in the cultures of the children in my classroom and how can I learn that language?" and "Is teaching in an urban school central to how I view myself as a teacher?" are the kinds of questions raised by teachers learning to incorporate the language demands of their settings into their professional identities.

BECOMING AN URBAN SCHOOLTEACHER

Sophie's dilemma, like those described by her colleagues Elsie, Laura, and Lucy, came from the tension she experienced figuring out who she was and who she wanted to be as an urban schoolteacher and what she believed was required or expected of her in her work. For all four teachers whose dilemmas we considered in this chapter, their goals and expectations reflect deeply held beliefs about themselves, their work, and their worlds. Like these brave teachers, most of us entered teaching with a set of beliefs about our work and ourselves without even realizing we had those beliefs. They are so much a part of our own personal history that we experience them simply as "the way things are" or even "the way things should be" without thinking too much about how our way of viewing the world might be different from those around us. In describing the challenges of learning to teach, LaBoskey (2004) points out that "Our beliefs, values and knowledge of teaching are derived from our experiences—our personal histories which are necessarily limited and variant" (p. 829). She reminds us further that "many of these assumptions are implicit; they have never been articulated even to us" (p. 829). As teachers we must come to understand ourselves—who we are and what we know and value—as well as what we believe about teaching and learning. These are the makings of our personal identity and the foundation on which we build the professional identity that will guide us in our work.

Palmer (1998), in his book *The Courage to Teach,* argues that understanding one's self, or the "self who teaches," is the starting point for developing a professional identity. He notes that most discussions of teaching begin with the questions of what to teach and how to teach it. His view is that a prior consideration in understanding teaching must be the question who is the self who teaches? Answers to the questions of what and how to teach are understood as reflections of the person making those decisions.

Beyond the teacher's sense of self are the social, cultural, historical, and political factors that surround teaching that also contribute to identity development in teachers. As we have seen in our consideration of the identity dilemmas in this chapter, the school context communicates to teachers what is expected (or not expected) of them in their role. This makes sense according to Wenger (1998) who posits identity as constructed within the context of social communities where meaning is determined and understood. Identity dilemmas arise for teachers when what is communicated to them from the context in which they work conflicts with how they view themselves as professionals. The teachers highlighted in this chapter all demonstrate how managing the dilemmas of teaching contributes to the development of a professional identity. As the teacher learns to anticipate the ways in which his or her sense of self as teacher is challenged by the demands of the context—and then to manage his or her practice in response—the teacher becomes an agent in his or her own professional identity formation (Florio-Ruane, 2002). As they manage the dilemmas of their practice, teachers whose personal histories do not include education in urban schools, and who are taken aback by demands that challenge their sense of themselves or their work, thus, begin to develop identities as urban schoolteachers.

CONCLUDING THOUGHTS

In this chapter we have considered how the urban school context raises professional-identity-development dilemmas for novice teachers. These dilemmas typically occur because the teachers' backgrounds and prior experiences are different from those they encounter in the schools where they teach. Whereas in this chapter we have considered teaching dilemmas of teachers of various races and ethnicities, the reality is that the majority of teachers in urban schools are White, while the majority of children in those schools are not (Zumwalt & Craig, 2005). Most White teachers are monolingual and speak only English, yet the majority of children in urban schools speak a language other than Standard English at home. Most teachers come from middle-class backgrounds, while many children in urban schools come from working-class or low-income households. The ideas, values, and beliefs novices bring with them to the profession reflect their backgrounds and the assumptions about teaching and learning. It is not uncommon for them to encounter ideas, values, and beliefs that differ from what they bring with them to the work. This then requires them to rethink what they have assumed to be true.

The continual process of learning to teach involves constructing and reconstructing this identity, as teachers encounter the realities of classroom life and the views of the profession shared by those with whom they come in contact in their work. Palmer (1998) writes, "Identity is a moving intersection of the inner and outer forces" that make a person who he or she is (p. 13). We saw this moving back and forth between inner and outer forces in each of the dilemmas presented here. We witnessed Sophie, questioning her professional identity as a bilingual teacher when she encountered the limits of her language knowledge. We encountered Elsie, grappling with her inner understanding of her African American identity and her students' conceptions of an African American identity. Lucy was caught between managing the outside reality of violence in her students' lives with her internal struggle to feel competent in the role of teacher. And Laura wrestled with conforming to the rules of standardized tests, all the while believing they were potentially hurtful to the children in her care. The managing of these dilemmas moved each of these teachers forward in understanding the work of teaching and understanding herself. Learning about both moved each forward toward becoming the teacher she wanted to become.

Learning to teach, which is a lifelong process, involves constructing and reconstructing one's identity as a teacher. The site where much of this learning occurs is the classroom, in which the teacher encounters both herself and the "external forces" of the context. As we have seen in the work of Lucy, Laura, Elsie, and Sophie, those encounters can generate tension for the teacher who is unsure what to do given the multiple choices she has for action. We have conceptualized these moments of tension as teaching dilemmas. Managing these dilemmas surfaces the teachers' beliefs and assumptions about teaching and learning and contributes to their ability to answer the important questions "Who am I?" and "Who do I want to become as teacher?"

CHAPTER 3

How Do I Care for Other People's Children?

Dilemmas About Students

> My knowledge of Ricky and his family in the early months of the
> year was comprised almost exclusively of "lacks." Ricky lacked
> sufficient reading skills; he lacked discipline at home; he lacked
> self-control and attentiveness; his mother lacked support. At
> that point it was primarily these "deficits" that characterized
> my understanding of him as a learner and determined my
> relationship with him as his teacher. What I lacked at this time
> was knowledge of his assets. I lacked an understanding of what
> he and his family *were* doing and what they *had*. I was not yet
> able to view his home and community. . . . In order to fulfill my
> moral obligation to teach Ricky to the best of my ability, I needed
> to know: what were his and his family's strengths. What funds of
> knowledge could contribute to his social and academic success?
>
> Sarah, *"Looking Deep"*[1]

In Chapter 2 we grappled with dilemmas associated with professional
identity formation. We saw how the process of deciding how to act when
facing a challenging decision that has no right answer requires looking inward to know "the self who teaches" (Palmer, 1998). This looking inward
surfaces our assumptions, beliefs, values, and commitments, and though
these may conflict with one another in the decision-making process, in
the end we must make a decision and act. The process leads teachers to
know themselves in their professional role.

At the same time the novices are learning about themselves as teachers, they must also learn about their students. The simultaneity of these
two processes adds to the complexity of each. Sarah, whose quote opens

this chapter, reveals the complex sense making teachers must do as they try to figure out who they are and who their students are at the same time. Sarah taught in a school that serves a population of poor children of color most of whose families were immigrants. She herself comes from a middle-class home and is Caucasian. We see in Sarah's reflection how learning about her student Ricky involved putting aside the assumptions and beliefs about his life that she brought with her to the classroom so that she could see him as he was, not as she assumed him to be. Only then would she be ready to serve him well.

As was true for Sarah, for many teachers in urban schools getting to know the students involves crossing both race and class lines and developing new lenses for understanding the students' experiences outside of school. This requires the teacher to de-center herself so that she can witness the reality of her students' lives. The process is particularly challenging for White, middle-class teachers who teach in schools where most students, like Ricky, are not White and not middle class. Teachers must learn to see the world as their students see it and develop a teaching practice that accounts for those important differences.

In writing about the work of identity formation and teaching, Martin Buber identified the potential difficulty of accomplishing this dual challenge of holding onto one's self while putting aside some of what one knows from one's past, to learn about the life experiences of others. He suggests that teachers must approach their students with a sense of "inclusiveness." Buber's biographer, Martin Friedman (1960), explains what Buber means by inclusiveness and how the student-teacher relationship thus conceived becomes a learning site for teachers. This inclusiveness, Friedman writes,

> is the essence of the dialogical relation, for the teacher sees the position of the other (the student) in his concrete actuality yet does not lose sight of his own. . . . Through discovering the 'otherness' of the pupil the teacher discovers his own real limits, but also through this discovery he recognizes the forces of the world which the child needs to grow and he draws those forces into himself. Thus, through his concern with the child, the teacher educates himself. (p. 177)

Understanding how much they do not know about their students' lives teaches teachers what they need to know to be successful working with them. We see in Sarah's account how learning about Ricky's life changed her relationship with him, the way she worked with him, and consequently both his success and hers. From engaging with our students and noting how they respond to us, teachers can also learn something about who they are as teachers and who they want to become.

LEARNING TO CARE FOR STUDENTS IN THE URBAN CONTEXT

Much of the teacher's learning about her students happens in a school context that shapes this learning in important ways. As we have discussed in chapters 1 and 2, there are characteristics of the urban setting that frame the lives of students and that challenge the teachers' learning about them. Importantly, it is often not the urban-school context itself that challenges teachers, but rather their preconceptions about urban schools constructed in part by a comparison with the prior school experiences that the novices bring with them to the work. In addition to their prior experiences, teachers encounter daily a profoundly limiting rhetoric about the urban-school setting. This impedes their learning as well. In the reflective essay Sarah wrote about her student Ricky, she recounted how the neighborhood schools where she taught were described to her before she arrived. She explained that while at her school teaching and learning were described in positive, hopeful, and exciting ways, when she heard others who were not directly part of her school community talk about the school their language was "suffused with deficit-laden descriptors of students, families, and urban communities" (Sugarman, 2008, p. 1). She explained that students were described as "'limited English proficient,' 'struggling,' and 'below grade-level.'" Families were described as "'overwhelmed,' 'checked out,' and 'confrontational.'" And the urban neighborhood was considered "'resource-deprived,' 'drug-infested,' and 'crime-ridden'" (p. 1).

Functioning in a context thus described made it difficult for Sarah in her position as a new teacher to keep such ideas at bay, especially, when faced with complex challenges in the unfamiliar school setting. Given how hard she was working and how little efficacy she felt, she found it difficult—sometimes painfully so—to hold on to the hope and promise of the children and families in her classroom. She wrote that the "mixture of social, emotional and academic needs" of her students overwhelmed her. Keeping her head above water required significant and constant effort. She explained, "I frequently felt incapable of addressing all the 'problems' and filling in all the 'gaps' that these 'limited English proficient,' 'struggling,' and 'below grade-level' students possessed" (p. 1). It took a deep desire to connect with her students, as well as focused outside support, for Sarah to embark on a journey of reframing her view of the lives of the families in her school to include their assets, strengths, and resources.

To illustrate her learning journey Sarah wrote about her student Ricky. She explained that before this reframing she viewed Ricky as hopelessly burdened by the challenges that poverty placed on him and his family. But by visiting him in his neighborhood and home and talking with his parents, Sarah began to see things in a different light. Rather than seeing Ricky as a child who "lacked reading skills, self control, and attentiveness," she began to recognize him as a child with considerable positive energy and talent whom she could help directly by drawing on his digital technology skills, his passion for and knowledge of cars, and his love of music. She also reframed her view of Ricky's mother focusing less on her job as a waitress in Jack in the Box and more as a young immigrant woman determined to support her son in achieving the best education her city's schools would offer. Sarah began to see Ricky and his family's lives as filled courage and conviction.

Most teachers enter the profession with a deep concern for students. In fact, teachers report that what brings them to teaching in the first place is their "love of children" or their "fascination with adolescents." Getting to know their students and establishing healthy, productive, relationships with them are high on the list of priorities for most of the teachers I know. And yet doing so can be difficult given some of the challenges we have been discussing—the teachers' lack of prior experience in urban settings, the challenges presented by crossing race and class lines, and the unconscious deficit view of urban children and schools that they have heard and perhaps unconsciously embraced. As teachers sort through these factors to both understand what it means to "care" for children in the context of school, they will undoubtedly run into uncertainties about what they should do. We turn now to the urban setting itself and some of the uncertainties it will predictably raise as teachers work to develop and sustain positive, productive student-teacher relationships.

KNOWING STUDENTS AND MEETING THEIR NEEDS

One challenge in developing healthy student-teacher relationships is assessing student needs, which is a difficult task for all teachers. For new teachers who are unfamiliar with the circumstances surrounding the lives of their students, making those needs assessments is more difficult still. As noted earlier, poverty and violence are two factors in urban settings that confound student-needs assessment for many teachers. Both get played out in school by students who arrive alienated by the circumstances of their lives, insecure due to their lack of preparation for academics, and/or confused by a system of education that they do not understand and that does not understand them. Knowing how to "read" students who are struggling in these ways coupled with the strong possibility of misreading them can paralyze teachers who want to do right on their students' behalf.

Consider the impact of poverty as an example. It is difficult to understand the experience or consequence of poverty when one has not been poor oneself. I am reminded of Nikki Giovanni's poem "Nikki-Rosa."[2] In this poem Giovanni points out how easy it is to get it wrong when interpreting other people's lives through one's own class, culture, and racial lenses. She worried about how those outside the experience of poverty conflate poverty with unhappiness, thus misrepresenting truth. Outsiders who write about growing up poor focus on the hardships, she explained, and "never talk about how happy you were to have your mother all to yourself and how good the water felt when you got your bath from one of those big tubs that folk in Chicago barbecue in."

As outsiders, it takes time to understand the lives of others. Even teachers who have the same background as their students are outsiders by virtue of their professional role. Giovanni helps us see that while children may find the work of school challenging, if they do not have enough food on their tables, or a sense of safety in walking to and from school, or a quiet place to study at home, they can be—and often are—happy. She reminds us that economic poverty does not mean emotional, spiritual, or intellectual poverty.

That said, poverty does impact children in significant ways that are important for teachers to understand (American Psychological Association, 2011; Berliner, 2009; Caldas & Bankston, 1997). If children come to school hungry they may have trouble concentrating enough to add fractions or interpret a complex text. If their parents both work the night shift and they need to get their younger siblings ready for school, they might arrive at school late themselves. High schoolers who have gone to under-resourced elementary and middle schools may not have the skill base they need to succeed when they get to high school. While learning about the obstacles poor children must overcome to feel welcome, safe, and successful in a place where they are afraid of being misunderstood, teachers must simultaneously commit to preparing them for academic success. Being poor does not mean one cannot be an excellent student. But overcoming the obstacles to learning that poverty presents renders becoming an excellent student difficult. Consider Josie's student, Bianca.

Josie's Dilemma

Josie teaches an English Language development class in a large, urban, public high school. All of her 22 students are English Language Learners (ELL). They came from 13 different countries and most had been here for a year or less. The families of these students were all struggling to make ends meet. Josie understood this. As the child of immigrants herself, she was aware of that struggle and supportive of students who had trouble concentrating in class, or who turned in assignments late. She understood how the stresses of life outside of school could not always be left at the classroom door. And at the same time, she was committed to insisting that her students learn English, follow school rules, and try hard to do good academic work. For her, the tension came from understanding the challenges her students faced in their lives outside of school while not compromising her expectations for their work in school. The student who brought this to life for Josie was Bianca.

> I have been particularly worried about one student in my class. Bianca has been absent and/or tardy a lot this semester. She doesn't turn in any work and barely does any classwork. She also seems to come to school looking like she cries before my class. At the beginning of the semester we talked about this and she explained to me that she was having "boyfriend drama." I didn't inquire further.

One day Bianca arrived 15 minutes late and seemed especially up-set. Josie asked her to stay at the end of class. The end of the marking period was approaching and she wanted to talk with Bianca about her attendance, her grade, and how she was doing in general. It was clear that something was wrong; this seemed like a good opportunity for her to see if she could better understand Bianca's struggles. She was particularly concerned that Bianca understand that her attendance and tardiness had consequences and that at that point she was failing the class. She also

wanted to tell Bianca that she and her partner teacher would be request-
ing a parent meeting to talk over the situation and see if there were ways
for Bianca's parents to help.

Bianca seemed relieved when Josie first asked to meet, but hearing
that her teachers wanted to meet with her parents, she burst into tears.
Her response alarmed Josie. Their conversation continued for an hour or
more, as Josie explained:

> During this hour she told me that she has many responsibilities at
> home which include cleaning and cooking before she leaves for
> school, and that is part of the reason why she comes to class late or
> doesn't show up at all. She continued to tell me that when these
> chores are not done to satisfaction she gets in a lot of trouble with
> her mother.

Josie learned also that Bianca's mother was under enormous stress herself, which meant that Bianca had to take on considerable responsibilities
at home to help. If she didn't complete the work in a way that her mom
thought was okay, her mother could become abusive. As Bianca's story
became more complex and troubling, Josie's anxiety grew about what she
should do to help.

Josie initiated this conversation with Bianca out of concern. Her goal
was to learn more about Bianca's life so that she could help her succeed
in school. The more she knew, however, the more confused she became
about what helping her would mean. Josie gained clarity from the conversation as to why Bianca had trouble making it to class and why she
was so distracted when finally she did arrive. Sadly, this clarity did not
extend to her knowing how to accomplish her coupled goals of caring for
Bianca while teaching her English. She could not accomplish either goal
if Bianca were not in class.

Confounding the situation further was Josie's legal obligation to report what was potentially a case of abuse. Bianca had bruises on her arms
and hands that she claimed were from her mother hitting her. If this were
true, Child Protective Services (CPS) needed to be contacted. But Josie
knew that Bianca was an undocumented immigrant. Though she had
heard from many reliable sources—including CPS itself—that CPS does
not check for citizenship status, she worried that this might not be true.
What if for some reason it were not true in this case? What would be the
consequences for Bianca and her mother of reporting the case? It could
easily make things even worse for them, and even mean deportation.

We can agree that learning about one's students is an important part of teaching them well. Understanding what they know, what they want to know, and what their prior experiences are all provide information that can be built upon in the classroom. But in many cases opening that door with students and learning about their lives only complicates an already complicated picture—at least in the short run. Also, as happened here with Bianca, it is possible that the teacher will learn things that then obligate her to take actions that she feels both uncertain about and unprepared to take. Weighing what she thinks she should do with what she feels obligated by law to do made Josie's decision about next steps especially challenging.

In Josie's case she had several important decisions to make, each attached to a dilemma that she had to reason through. One involved whether or not to report Bianca's case to CPS. On the one hand, she was legally obligated to do so. But doing so could have had serious negative consequences for Bianca and her family. Another decision involved whether to hold Bianca to the same attendance standards she had for Bianca's classmates. If Josie held Bianca to a standard she could not meet, she might give up and drop out of school altogether, as so many of her peers had done. In their city, close to 50% of the students who enrolled in high school at 9th grade dropped out before graduation. Josie did not want Bianca to be another dropout statistic, but to not hold her to the attendance standard would mean lowering her expectations for Bianca, which she did not want to do either.

At the time of this writing, Josie had not decided what actions to take. She was not clear what to do about her legal obligation to report the suspected abuse. She was also unclear what to do about Bianca's lack of attendance. By sharing her dilemma with her colleagues, she realized that she need not be alone in making the decision, which she said was a great relief. Though teachers feel sequestered in their own classrooms and may feel isolated, they need not be. Teacher colleagues and school leaders can help them sort through the difficult decisions they must make such as the decisions facing Josie. Her case helps us see why as a profession we must make those avenues of collaboration more open and obvious to all teachers. This work of managing dilemmas is too complex for one person to do alone.

Josie wanted to help Bianca become a better student so that she would be successful at learning English. When she began to explore what was getting in the way of Bianca's learning, she uncovered a set of circumstances about Bianca's life that made knowing how to help her more confusing. Learning to act with an ethic of care, which involves determining what kind of care and how much is appropriate, are all part of teaching and learning to teach. While the details are different from one teacher and situation to another, the journey of getting to know one's students and then building a curriculum and instructional plan that takes into account what one learns from that investigation are part of what it means to teach. But the decisions the teacher needs to make are seldom easy, as Josie's account makes clear.

As teachers work to get to know their students and establish relationships with them, they often find themselves pondering how much help their students need and what kind of help. They want their students to feel welcome and confident so that they are able to take the risks associated with learning and eventually assume responsibility for their own learning when the direct caring support of the teacher is removed. The judgment call is often difficult. I have heard many teachers—new and veteran alike—ask, "How much help should I provide and when might that help get in the way of the student's learning or the learning of the other students in the class?" It was this question that was at the heart of Serena's dilemma about how to respond to her student Marshall.

Serena's Dilemma

Serena teaches high school English in an urban school that mostly serves Latino/a and South East Asian students. Her dilemma concerned her student Marshall, the only African American boy in her 10th grade multiracial classroom in this working-class community. "Physically," Marshall "is the largest student in the class," she wrote. "Socially he is the most isolated. Academically he is the furthest behind." Marshall sought out Serena by arriving early to class most days to talk with her about her plans for the day and telling her which parts of the lesson he thought he'd do and "which parts he wouldn't." He also shared with her things about his life. She wrote, "He talks with me regularly about being one of the only Black students, about being the biggest one, and about preferring to sit alone or work alone." She engaged with him, she explained, by "good-naturedly" joining in, "consciously responding in a positive and encouraging way that lets him know I believe he can do it (whatever it may be) but that ultimately he has the choice of doing or not doing the work that it takes to succeed in the class."

Serena wrote that all the while she spent encouraging Marshall she wondered to herself if it really were possible for him to be successful in her class, not because of his innate ability to do the work, but because of his prior academic preparation—or lack of it. She pondered, "Inside me there lurks a voice that knows that in many ways he does not have a true choice" to succeed, at least without "super-human" effort. She wondered what that super-human effort would look like and how her role as teacher would or could impact it. She also wondered if his lack of preparation were the only barrier Marshall faced in doing the work or if he might have had a learning disability. She does not know how to judge this herself and her school does not have the resources for someone else to help.

Whatever the reason, Marshall arrived in Serena's class seriously underprepared. It didn't take long for her to realize that he did not have the requisite skills to engage with the class assignments. But she was determined to help him overcome his lack of preparation by consistently encouraging him to do the work and by helping him fill in his answers with extra coaching. All the while she worried that his chances for success were dim, something he seemed to recognize as well. Watching his push and pull with her—"I'll do the work or maybe I won't"—led Serena to imagine how it would feel to be encouraged to do work for which you have neither the needed prior skills or knowledge. His behavior made more and more sense to her over time. She wrote,

> I suspect that he has resisted what he sees as attempts to force him to work and suffer and probably not succeed anyway, and that his resistance has been stronger than the educational system's supposed drive to help him succeed.

Serena and her partner teacher remained determined to help Marshall. But gradually they began to wonder at what cost. Though they managed to help him maintain a D in the class, Serena was not sure how much he was learning. She began to wonder if she and her partner teacher were helping so much that in the end Marshall's work reflected more of their thinking than it did his. She questioned how much help in this way was actually helpful and if, instead, it might be getting in the way of his getting the help he really needed. She began to realize that what would help Marshall was "a more sophisticated and nuanced assessment" of his learning and academic needs and, then, a targeted plan for addressing them. Given that the school did not provide that service, she agonized over what she should do.

In the meantime, Serena's dilemma regarding Marshall raised a second dilemma, this one concerned the rest of her class. She worried about how much time she was spending helping Marshall—and how little time she had left to work with her other students. She explained that her focus on Marshall reflected her concern for him, in part, "because he represents to me a population of students that historically gets the short end of the stick when these sorts of dilemmas arise." At the same time her belief that she was spending an "unfair amount of time with him" was exacerbated by the nagging worry that no matter how much time she spent, it would not be enough.

Serena described a litany of questions about how best to serve Marshall and her other students at the same time. She wondered if giving Marshall this help was getting in the way of his receiving the support he really needed for academic success. She questioned whether spending individualized time with him might prevent him from developing the social skills that would help him feel less isolated or might make him dependent on her thinking rather than his own. She questioned as well whether it was ethical to push her notions of success on him without exploring the type of success he wanted. Constantly in the back of her mind were the other students and what the consequences of her attention on Marshall were for their learning.

Serena's dilemma regarding Marshall raised the question of boundaries, a predictable challenge for teachers. Because all students need the teacher's attention and many will ask for it, it is important for teachers to establish and maintain boundaries that support student growth. It's easy to get pulled away from the needs of the whole group by a student who is especially needy, or especially demanding (or both). In the urban setting, which may be unfamiliar to the teacher, or even for teachers who are familiar with this setting—where many children appear to need considerable support—managing the demands in a way that is balanced is an important professional skill. Serena wanted to address Marshall's needs and help him achieve success; at the same time she was also concerned about her other students. There will always be some students who, for various reasons, require more time and attention than others. All students deserve their teacher's attention. Finding ways to care for each child in the class and not only those who demand attention is a persistent challenge.

The relationship Serena established with Marshall was born of a concern, as she said, of "better serving traditionally underserved students" whose need for extra support was clearly evident. In urban settings there are typically many students who are underprepared for the work they are asked to do. Some of this is due to students arriving in these classrooms with little academic preparation from the countries they had lived in before arriving in the United States. Some of the lack of preparation is due to poverty and the financial strain on families that makes supporting the academic development of their children extremely difficult. This is exacerbated when the parents themselves are the products of the same struggling school system and do not have the academic skills to help their children and, further, when these schools lack resources for students with special needs.

VIOLENCE AND CARE FOR STUDENTS IN URBAN SCHOOLS

Violence is an additional factor that looms heavy over urban schools. The issue of violence is not restricted to urban schools—in fact, we have witnessed in recent years acts of school violence in both suburban and rural settings. That said, the level of violence in urban communities in general is a constant concern for teachers. Most children in urban classrooms are familiar with violence, as they have seen it on the streets where they live. The sound of gunshots and the experience of violent death are not unfamiliar to many children who attend schools in poor urban neighborhoods. How to care for children who bring with them to school fears and other feelings associated with the violence they have witnessed raises dilemmas for teachers—especially for teachers who have little experience with violence themselves.

Emily's Dilemma

Emily teaches a 3rd-grade class of 19 students in a working-class neighborhood. Ten of her students are African American; six, Mexican; two, Indian; and one, Korean. Her dilemma concerned her student Cameron, a lively African American boy who struggled to stay focused and keep up with the work in class. His reading was below grade level and he demonstrated little self-confidence. He lived near the school with his mother, his sister, and his older brother, all of whom he talked about frequently. Whereas he had a "sensitive side," Emily wrote, he caused quite a bit of disruption in class by calling out and saying "nasty things to his classmates."

Emily's concern for Cameron centered on her feeling that every day he was slipping further and further behind in his work. Among the strategies she and her partner teacher devised to address this concern was to have Emily work with him individually during reading while the rest of the class worked in book groups. Their hope was that one-on-one attention might help Cameron with his reading and build his self-confidence at the same time. It would also provide Emily an opportunity to monitor his reading and develop a better understanding of the challenges he faced in making sense of what he read. In addition, time with Cameron would provide Emily an opportunity to get to know him better and see beyond his disruptive behavior.

As the individual work got underway, Cameron began to share with Emily the personal side of his life. She began to see him in his full humanity as a sensitive child trying to make his way in a complex world. Weeks passed and Emily's relationship with Cameron grew. Her dilemma came one day when she and Cameron were reading a chapter in the book *Doggone Third Grade* about a talent show in a 3rd-grade classroom like Cameron's. Gordie, the story's protagonist lived an exciting life, which drew Cameron in just as Emily hoped it would. Gordie had lots of fun after school riding on his father's motorcycle, pretending to be a cop. When Emily asked Cameron if "he had any connections he could make to what he had just read," he replied, "Yes, I do. We have an abandoned car in the alleyway at our house. I play cops and robbers with my brother after school. We pretend to have guns and shoot each other." Another gun story, Emily thought to herself; at this point these were becoming commonplace in their exchanges.

In spite of her nagging concern for his fascination with guns, Emily felt good about Cameron's progress. He was engaged in the reading and she was getting to know him in a new way. Yet she was worried at the same time. Whenever the chance arose, he shared another gun story with her—some real and some fictional. She was never sure which were which. There had been recent stories of violence in his neighborhood, including a number of shootings, which she knew were making her especially sensitive. "But shouldn't I be hypersensitive given this?" she asked herself. Meanwhile, Cameron expressed so much enthusiasm in sharing his story about the cops and robbers game he played with his brother that she was reluctant to bring up her gun concern for fear of shutting him down. After all, she thought, lots of boys his age like to play cops and robbers. And she wanted him to feel that he could bring his home experiences to school.

Putting her concern aside about his fascination with guns, Emily decided to begin her conversation with Cameron about his response to the story, complimenting him on making a personal connection by talking about what he does after school. He seemed happy to have pleased her, which opened the door for him to tell more about his life including about his sister, who was about to get out of jail. He said, "Do you know my sister is getting out of jail this month? Ms. C., maybe if I am good and behave at school you can buy me a gun so I can protect her from her enemies."

Emily felt her "stomach drop." She wrote, "I didn't know what to say." Gathering herself, she told him that she would never buy him a gun, explaining that guns "do bad things" and "should only be used by policemen to protect people." Cameron appeared to be confused and Emily could see why. He may have thought that as policemen's guns are meant to protect, his gun would be to protect his sister also. Emily continued, "desperately trying to give Cameron the message that violence was not the answer." The reading time was over and Emily felt Cameron looked relieved to see his classmates lining up to go to lunch. He asked Emily if he could leave, and with her permission, he scooted off to the playground. Meanwhile, she wrote,

> I stayed at the red table trying to process what Cameron had just told me. Should I tell my partner teacher about the conversation? Or should I just keep it between the two of us? Perhaps Cameron was confiding in me. After about 5 minutes I stood up, took a deep breath and walked into the classroom.

Emily's dilemma was not about how to respond to Cameron's request. It took her only a few seconds to gather her thoughts and respond. The dilemma came in deciding what to do with this information and how to manage her more general concern for his safety. As teachers establish trusting relationships with their students, they learn more about them, which helps them teach them well. As we saw in Josie's case about Bianca, given the complexities of students lives, some of what teachers learn as these relationships grow is privileged information students do not want them to share. In Emily's case, Cameron did not ask Emily to keep his request for a gun private. But Emily still wondered if she should tell someone about this—and who? Was Cameron just talking "kids' talk," or was there something in his message that was real and should be of concern? Was he safe? She framed her dilemma, "Do I sacrifice breaking the trust I spend so much time to build with a student—for serving the duty I have as a teacher to keep my students safe?" She continued, "It sounds so easy to answer on paper, but when you are in the thick of it and so much is at stake, it's really a hard decision to make."

In reasoning through her dilemma Emily realized how clear she was about the importance of her relationship with Cameron. She wrote, "On the one hand, I saw all my effort in establishing this relationship come to fruition in this incident. Cameron was confiding in me. He trusted me!" She felt that if she told someone else about this, Cameron would feel betrayed. She wrote, "As a believer that teaching happens in the context of a relationship, I just did not want to sacrifice that relationship. . . . Without that relationship, what did I have?" Emily had a clear goal of getting to know Cameron and establishing a relationship with him within which he would be willing to take the risks needed to learn new things. Teaching takes place in the context of a relationship, as Emily noted. So does learning. At the same time, Emily realized her role as teacher and her responsibility for Cameron's safety. "I felt that the things Cameron was talking about put him in an unsafe zone." Emily did not want to compromise the newly formed and perhaps fragile relationship, and at the same time, she needed to do her best to keep him safe.

Violence as a part of the urban context impacts the relationships teachers have with their students and raises dilemmas concerning the competing dimensions of what it means to act with an ethic of care. For both Rachel, whose student told a story about scaring another boy and making him jump (Chapter 1), and Emily, whose case we have just reviewed, the dilemmas came in how to respond to the innocent expressions of violence that involve their students doing the everyday work of school. Hawkins (2002) would explain that it was in mutual engagement in the subject matter that formed the relationships Emily and Rachel had with their students. It was in this safe relational context that included provocative subject matter that the children felt free to reveal some of the realities of their lives. In both cases these students were already struggling in school. The relationships with their teachers provided them a way to engage and bring their lives outside of school with them through the classroom door; it was through their engagement with their teachers and their subject matter that they found a way to talk about what was going on in their lives. It was only then that their schoolwork began to improve.

Establishing a classroom environment that makes it safe for children to talk about their world and to connect that world of home to their schoolwork is critical if school is to become welcoming and meaningful for students. If children can engage by sharing stories of their families and lives outside of school—and thus get a sense that their lives "matter"—the chance that they will engage with the academic work of school increases. Hearing their stories helps teachers expand their understanding of their students' lives. Violence is part of the life of many children in urban settings. Learning about the impact of violence on children can help teachers anticipate what might come up if their students are truly engaged in their work. With this advance thinking, teachers can be better prepared to know what to do when they are successful in creating a safe place where their students can talk—and do talk—about the realities of their lives. In addition to the challenges raised by poverty and violence, we might also ask ourselves what else is going on in the communities where we teach that we can anticipate that our students will bring with them to school. How can we prepare ourselves for those eventualities as well?

We have argued thus far that teachers need to learn as much as they can about the students' lives outside of school so they can draw on that knowledge when they are teaching. If poverty and violence are part of the child's life outside of school, the more teachers know about both, and the impact of both on children, the better they will be at doing their work. They will be less often caught off guard by their students' actions, and they will be more likely to create a classroom where children feel cared for and safe enough to participate. However, knowing about violence and its potential impact on children's lives is only a starting point for knowing how to deal with violence successfully. Felipe's dilemma makes that point in a very clear way.

Felipe's Dilemma

Unlike the cases we have studied thus far, Felipe grew up in the neighborhood where he teaches. Whereas he described his school as an "angry" place, for him it was not an unfamiliar place. And in spite of the troubled larger school context he felt he had been able to make his 7th-grade humanities class of 30 students (24 Latino/a, 4 African American, and 2 Tongan) a place where students had learned to respect one another. Felipe believed that a good part of this respect came from the shared background he had with his students and the relationships he developed with them over the school year. He wrote,

> Due to my own experience I feel as if I can relate to many of the students . . . I feel as if I have a strong rapport with them. They tell

me stories of their lives on the streets. In addition, I listen to their conversations and watch their interactions with each other as well as other students in the school.

Even with all of his prior knowledge about the neighborhood and the school, Felipe found himself struggling with a dilemma born from the violence that existed in his community. His concern was for one of his students, Julio. He felt he had a good relationship with Julio and was troubled when he observed him beginning to engage in what he thought might be dangerous behavior. Though he felt he knew Julio, he wrote, "Nothing thus far had prepared me for the situation I encountered during the last month."

Felipe's dilemma began when, parking his car one morning, he witnessed just outside the school fence Julio, his "100 lb. 7th-grade student," being held to the ground by Sergio, a large, hefty gang member. Standing by to watch this event were several other students all known to be in gangs—one, who had been recently kicked out of school for being caught with a firearm, and a second, who was suspended for drawing graffiti on the school walls. Felipe sat stunned. Watching closely it appeared to him that Sergio was not hurting Julio. He wanted to intervene, but worried that if he did he might be putting Julio in more danger. So he watched to be certain Julio was okay and then made the decision not to approach him right then, which might embarrass him in front of his bigger and more powerful friends. When they dispersed, he left, resolving to talk with Julio in private later in the day.

After class, Felipe asked Julio to stay for a minute to ask him how he was doing. He told him that he had seen him with Sergio before school and that it looked like a rough encounter. He offered to give him a ride home. Julio declined.

Felipe was concerned and wondered what he should do. He felt that Julio was not himself and that his silence was a signal that something was wrong. He felt Julio trusted him and he wanted to be of help if Julio needed help, but he didn't want to overstep a boundary if there was no reason to do so. He thought perhaps if he approached Julio the next day, after they had both had time to think about what had occurred, Julio might open up. At the same time, he didn't want to create tension, which might cause him to close down more. All the while he could not erase the image of Julio with Sergio and the other gang members. He felt he could not let things go further without taking some kind of action.

When Felipe arrived at school the next day, he found a note on his desk that said, "Don't mess with us b**tch, don't you know we're the South Side Locos?" It warned, "Watch your back b**tch!" and was signed by El Vato X3.

The note left Felipe shocked, troubled, and scared. He knew the note was likely written by a gang member, and one probably involved in the incident he had witnessed with Julio the day before. He worried that it could possibly be from Julio but he thought not. He approached a colleague to get some support and advice, which was helpful though together they were no clearer as to what Felipe should do. They agreed that it was unlikely that Julio would write such a note or that he would be in a gang.

A week later Felipe called Julio in to talk with him about his reading journal on which was drawn a bubbled number 13, a symbol Felipe knew to be associated with gangs. He asked Julio why he drew this and why he included it in his journal. Julio shrugged his shoulders and otherwise did not reply. Felipe wrote, "I repeated the question again in a soft, unthreatening voice" and again he only shrugged his shoulders. He persisted by asking Julio if he was being pressured to join a gang and suggested he talk with the school counselor, but Julio remained silent. Felipe said, "I gave him a couple of anonymous hotlines that would allow him to call for advice. He seemed surprised, so I just ripped the page out of his journal and then ripped the page in half again." Leaning on the relationship he thought he had with Julio, Felipe ended the meeting telling him how much this made him worry about him. "Don't draw this symbol ever again because it makes me worry about you. Know how much I care about you."

Felipe's concern for Julio's safety continued, as did the consistent rebuffs Julio gave in return. Julio kept his distance, avoiding Felipe whenever possible. In the meantime, several additional threatening notes appeared on Felipe's desk. As the situation escalated, Felipe knew he had to take additional steps. He spoke with both the school principal and counselor; eventually all eyes were on Julio, watching carefully. Felipe then made the hard decision to call Julio's mother. Since his efforts at connecting with Julio had thus far failed and his concern for Julio's safety continued to grow, notifying his family seemed necessary. He figured they may know more about Julio's life outside of school and, if they did not, knowing that Julio might be in danger would be important. At the same time Felipe expected that contacting his mother would push Julio even further away—that he would see it as an act of betrayal. But since Julio was not sharing any information with him and he could not let go of the possibility that Julio was in danger, Felipe decided it would be a greater betrayal to not include his family at this point.

Julio's mother was shocked to hear that Julio was in trouble. She was equally shocked that Sergio was a member of a gang. "Sergio is the only friend that I allow Julio to hang out with . . . he is a good kid. He's had dinner with our family."

After the conversation with Julio's mother, Felipe received a third note, which had his "name crossed out and ten block numbers around my home crossed out as well." Felipe's concern for Julio's safety spread to a concern for his own safety. The third threatening note led to an all-out investigation. Ultimately it was determined that Julio was the author of these notes and eventually he admitted to writing them. Julio's mother was as surprised and upset as was Felipe. When Julio was asked why he wrote the notes, he said "I did it because he made me mad. He accused me of being a gangster."

Felipe's case demonstrates how complicated it is to establish relationships with students whose lives are framed day in and day out by violence. Gangs are not an inconsequential threat to children in urban schools. The amount of gang activity in most of our urban centers is well documented (Herrenkohl et al., 2000). Gangs reflect both the child's need for affiliation and the reality of violence in our communities (Howell & Decker, 1999).

This experience impacted Felipe as we can only imagine it would. It raised questions for him about his own vulnerability and safety. In sorting it through he pondered how paramedics and lifeguards learn that in an unsafe situation one might not be able to help a victim because doing so might make him or her a victim as well. He asked, "Should a teacher not involve himself in gang-related cases? Is that putting your safety at risk too? Does it mean you have to come to terms with the fact that your student is in a gang and endangering himself?" Reflecting on this experience with Julio and what he knew about life in his community he wrote, "After all, once a student has joined a gang, there is no way out without severe or irreparable harm to the student or his or her family."

Felipe's dilemma began with a student with whom he felt he had already established a relationship. The dilemma came in realizing how fragile that relationship was in a context in which other factors, such as gang membership and violence, draw on a child's vulnerabilities. Felipe's knowledge of the community where he has returned to teach made him vulnerable as well. From the beginning he read the situation with Julio in ways others of us may have missed. He knew firsthand about the struggles kids face and the temptations that are part of their everyday lives. He chose to teach in this community because of his deep concern and care for the children who lived there. On the one hand, he remained committed to protect them as best he could. At the same time, he learned through this painful experience, how difficult and potentially dangerous it could be to do so.

CONCLUDING THOUGHTS

In this chapter we have considered how important it is to get to know one's students, and how difficult that work can be when the realities of the context impact the students' lives in particularly challenging ways. A guiding idea for the chapter is that establishing caring relationships with students is central to teaching them well. The process begins with finding ways to learn about students beyond the work they do in our classrooms. The process builds our capacity for establishing relationships with students where they can see that we care about them. If trust is established, students are more likely to take the risks associated with learning.

Whereas creating an opportunity for the student to be in a caring relationship with the teacher is itself an important goal of teaching, the goal of creating a relational context within which the student can learn and develop academically in school, must also be at the forefront of the teacher's mind. For all students, especially students in high needs, under-resourced schools that serve high percentages of poor and/or immigrant children, receiving an education is the best—and for some, the only—hope for a future in which one can support oneself and become a contributing member of a family and community. If receiving that education depends in part on the kinds of relationships students have with their teachers, the centrality of building those relationships becomes clear.

Getting to know one's students and then using that knowledge to guide one's teaching are not straightforward processes, however. As we can see from the cases considered here, there are predictable dilemmas teachers will face about what actions to take at almost every point in the process. Teachers will always find themselves asking such questions as these: What do I need to know about my students? How can I find those things out without violating my student's privacy? Are there cultural norms I should be aware of before asking students about their lives? Are there things I would be better off not knowing if I am to serve this student well? All of these questions, and more like them can paralyze a teacher. So, too, can the questions that arise once the teacher has learned about the student's life and then wonders how what she or he has learned should influence the work with that student: Should I hold Bianca to the same attendance standards as my other students? Should I talk to Cameron's mother about his wanting to get a gun? Should I confront Julio directly now that I've seen him hanging around with known members of a gang? Finding out about the out-of-school lives of our students impacts our ability to teach them. In spite of the challenges and questions that arise as we take on this task, take it on we must.

All of the teachers whose cases we considered in this chapter entered teaching with a deep commitment to learn about the lives of their students. All of them made good progress at making that occur. In every case, and in the many cases like them, the process raised dilemmas that required soul searching to determine how to best draw on what they knew about their students' lives when deciding the action to take that would be in the students' best interest. These decisions for action are seldom clear for teachers, but committing to the process of framing the dilemma, reasoning it through, and then acting according to what the teacher believes is best for the student are central.

As we move forward in considering the dilemmas of teaching, we can put learning about students and knowing what to do with that knowledge high on our list. Thinking about these dilemmas in advance and knowing that they will present themselves when one begins to teach will, it is hoped, provide a starting point for knowing how to manage them and take action. Sometimes the action one takes doesn't have the expected outcome. This becomes an opportunity for the teacher to learn about that student, in particular, and to learn about students in general. Reasoning through the dilemmas that face one as teacher, taking action, and learning from the outcome are solid means for becoming a teacher who knows his or her students and can use that knowledge to help them succeed in school.

CHAPTER 4

What Should I Teach and How?

Curriculum and Instruction Dilemmas

I feel very strongly that curriculum should meet and connect with
the experiences of the students in a class. Every student should
feel like his/her history/experience/culture is represented in some
way. I promised my classes that we will look at Native Americans,
Asian Americans, Irish, Filipino, and German (specific groups
that they requested learning about), but I also feel that a true
multicultural education is concerned with social justice and thus
exposes students to and creates empathy for oppressed groups. I
cannot not teach about African Americans, but it seems like when
I do I am arousing racist sentiments rather than squelching them.
How do I get students to be able to step into the shoes of the
other ethnic groups and see why it is so important to understand
power if we are going to understand culture? How do I do this as
an outsider to these oppressed groups? And how do I teach about
cultures for which I have no curriculum and [about which I have]
very little of my own knowledge? Help!!!

Karina, *"Where to begin"*

No sooner than the new teachers find themselves in the classroom will
they have to decide what to teach—and how to teach it. The questions
of what and how to teach are not far distant from those of identity and
student-teacher relationships that we have considered thus far. Faced
with the challenge of deciding what to teach, the teacher will confront
his or her own uncertainty or lack of knowledge as we see in Karina's
quote above. New to her school and her classroom, Karina felt paralyzed
by the challenge of creating what she hoped would be an inclusive curriculum for her 9th graders, most of whom actively resisted her attempts
to do so. The class Cultures and Identities was an elective offered to

students who had completed their other requirements. Those choosing it were from the "high track." In spite of the high percentage of students of color in Karina's school, with the exception of two second-generation Latinos and one Native American, the remaining students in her class were half White and half Asian. It appeared that the class was tracked by race as well as academic achievement.

Karina explained that because the class was an elective, "I have a lot of freedom to teach what I want," which turned out to be both a bonus and a challenge. It was also the catalyst for her dilemma. The freedom gave her the opportunity to create a curriculum and classroom culture that reflected her goals as a teacher. But it didn't provide the knowledge she needed to be able to do so in a way that would meet her students' needs especially in the face of their unexpected and determined resistance.

From the outset Karina set out to create a classroom culture in which all voices were welcome; she listened to the students as she expected them to listen to her. Establishing healthy and productive relationships with students was high on her list of priorities. To contribute to that goal she wanted her curriculum to be inclusive and draw from her students' experiences—something she had learned to consider in her professional preparation program. Teaching in a diverse urban school, she was especially sensitive to making sure the curriculum reflected the life experiences of all of the students in the school. She wanted her students to develop empathy for people who were different from them and hoped her class would be one in which students would learn about the other communities of students, in particular, those communities not represented in their class. Given that the class demographics were different from the demographics of her school, she thought she might be able to help students develop a critical consciousness starting with a collective consideration of the dearth of Latino/a and African American students in this class and in the high-track classes in general.

However, Karina's plans were quickly foiled when she presented them to her students. Upon sharing the course syllabus, indicating the inclusion of several pieces of literature by African American authors, the students complained that they were "sick" of hearing about African Americans. She was upset by their reaction and stymied regarding how to proceed. She wanted to confront them immediately and make it clear that such comments were not acceptable in her classroom. At the same time, she did not want to set up an adversarial relationship with them the first day of school. She reminded herself that they were 14-year-olds and at a critical point in their identity development. It made sense that they wanted to learn about their own histories and cultures. From their point of view, studying their histories and backgrounds was seldom part of the curriculum in their highly diverse school. As they experienced their school's attempt at inclusion, studying about African Americans was everywhere. They wanted the curriculum to be "fair" and include studying their families' histories as well.

Karina remembered reading that providing students an "opportunity to explore and study the history, culture, literature and other intellectual products of members of their racial or ethnic group can have a positive effect on the development of students' racial or ethnic identity" (Zirkel, 2008). It made sense that this would be true for White and Asian students just as it was for children who are African American or Latin American. At the same time, she wanted to help her students see the imbalance that existed in the school's curriculum, noting that the study of Euro-American history and culture covers most of what we find in the standard school curriculum. She hoped to turn their resistance into a "teachable moment," when she and the group could together analyze how much of the social studies curriculum and even the curriculum of the school more broadly focused on the experience of White Americans in spite of the school's demographics.

How to respond to her students and at the same time hold on to her deep commitment to develop and teach an inclusive curriculum sets the stage for this chapter's consideration of curriculum and instruction dilemmas. While Karina's dilemma surfaces in the domain of curriculum, it has embedded in it both identity and student-teacher relationship concerns. Creating an inclusive curriculum was core to who Karina felt she was as a teacher. She saw her curriculum as an enactment of who she wanted to be in her new professional role. The challenge to hold onto her strong commitment to interrupt what she perceived to be racism in her classroom was tied to her identity as a social studies teacher committed to equity, justice, and change. At the same time, being responsive to her students and establishing positive productive relationships with them were also part of what she hoped to accomplish in her new role. Managing those two seemingly conflicting goals was at the heart of the curriculum dilemma presented here.

In considering Karina's dilemma, we can see how intertwined the challenges are that teachers face. To make decisions about what to teach, teachers find themselves considering their beliefs about what is most worth knowing and balancing that with what they think are the expectations of their job, as defined by the different stakeholders (including students). As we will see in the pages that follow, the curriculum in the diverse context of the urban school typically involves a negotiation—explicit or not—between the teacher and the student. As the students engage with the curriculum presented by the teacher, they construct their own knowledge and raise questions that often take the teacher in directions she had not planned to go. This makes it all the more important for teachers to be clear about both their own values and commitments and also what they know about the students they will teach.

A third factor in the curriculum negotiation process in urban schools is the set of district, state, and in some instances national guidelines that outline what teachers should teach and what students should learn. Interestingly, state standards and requirements were not part of Karina's dilemma since the class she was teaching was an elective. But for many—perhaps most teachers in high-needs, urban settings—state regulations and standardized tests constrain curricular choices. By virtue of being constructed outside the context where they are to be implemented, these external forces raise dilemmas for teachers who aim to create a curriculum that is responsive to the lives of the students they see everyday.

TEACHER AS CURRICULUM DEVELOPER

Curriculum development—deciding what and how to teach—is at the heart of good teaching. Even with everything else teachers must do, such as creating a welcoming classroom environment, talking with parents, getting to know students, keeping attendance records, and attending faculty meetings, at the center of it all is preparing, enacting, and assessing a curriculum designed to teach the content, skills, and dispositions students need to have productive and happy lives. The process begins with deciding what to teach and is followed closely by how to teach it. But deciding what and how to teach is not easy—not for beginners or for veteran teachers. New teachers may be comforted to know that they are not alone in the struggle to decide both what their students should learn and how they should teach those things, and also what their role is in making those choices. All teachers grapple with these questions—especially those for whom it appears there is little discretion in making curricular choices. These questions of curriculum are not new. History teaches us that they have been of central concern in American education for centuries (Cremin, 1964; Kleibard, 1995; Oakes & Lipton, 2003).

Politics is one reason curriculum decision making in the urban school context is so challenging. The enduring political debate about curriculum in U.S. schools harkens back to the basic question of purpose: What are schools for? Who should be taught what and how? Who should decide? Questions such as whether or not all students should learn the same things and be taught in the same ways have persisted in the field since public education began, yet these questions are important today because of the diversity of the student population especially in urban public schools. In spite of current legislation that mandates various forms of standardization including a common curriculum of core subjects to be taught in a standard or paced way, teachers who face today's multicultural, multilingual class-rooms continue to ask themselves what content is appropriate for which students, how to teach all of them the content that is mandated, and how to incorporate their students' funds of knowledge and ways of knowing into their curricular plans.

CURRICULUM DEVELOPMENT IN THE URBAN CONTEXT— RESPONDING TO DIVERSITY

The process of curriculum development begins with choosing what to teach. In recent years, the teachers' role in determining the content of instruction has diminished given external guidelines that constrain their choices. Schools that serve communities of poverty are typically those that score low on the academic performance index (API). They are, thus, labeled low performing and, as a consequence, bear the burden of high levels of external control and regulation, including standardized curricular and instructional choices as well as standardized tests. These strategies—standardizing the curriculum, instruction, and testing—are meant to ensure that all students receive comparable opportunities to learn. They are strategies designed to promote equity. Many argue that the outcomes of these measures, however, yield opposite results (Popham, 2001; Ravitch, 2010). One reason for this can be attributed to the challenges faced by teachers in these settings given the wide range of prior experiences, including academic skills, that their students hold when the school year begins. Another reason is that the student popula-tion in urban schools is becoming increasingly diverse, which suggests that less rather than more standardization may be needed. In any case, the restrictions placed on teachers predictably raise dilemmas for them. A teacher faces a challenging dilemma when she wants (and needs) to teach what is being asked of her, on the one hand, but believes that a different curriculum and instructional plan would work better for the students on the other.

Even with considerable external control, however, in most instances teachers still have a role in shaping the curriculum they teach day to day. Knowing how to make those instructional choices and how to negotiate the curricular terrain given the external regulation and pressure are important. The teacher in these instances must keep in mind the responsibility of preparing students for the challenges ahead including the standardized tests they will encounter, which are gateways to future opportunities. At the same time the teacher must also learn to balance what is "required" to teach with what he or she believes she "ought" to teach given what he or she knows about the students, including who they are, what they already know, and what is valued in their communities. Consider Zelda's struggle.

Zelda's Dilemma

Zelda teaches 3rd grade in an urban elementary school. Of her 20 students, 13 are Black, and 7 are White. Her dilemma occurred in the middle of her social studies unit when, following the school's 3rd-grade social studies curriculum, she was teaching the Underground Railroad. As she planned the unit she struggled to decide what aspect of this period of history and the Underground Railroad she wanted to include. Her plan was to teach Harriet Tubman and the brilliant way Tubman worked with others to bring her people to the North and freedom. This was the approach taken by the other 3rd-grade teachers at her school and as a new teacher she did not want to step outside any curricular (or political) lines. At the same time, she felt strongly that she wanted to teach history in a balanced and honest way, which led her to think hard about how to teach this time period and not gloss over the realities of the slave experience by focusing solely on Harriet Tubman and her extraordinary courage. She was determined to not teach what she considered "watered down truths." She pondered the latter part of the 18th century in American history, keeping in mind that this was a period of trauma and violence for many living in the South. She felt that to not present this as part of the picture limited her students' possible understanding of what the Underground Railroad was about.

Zelda's dilemma came to a head during a class discussion about the slave experience that was the impetus for the Underground Railroad, when one of the Black students asked, "Why didn't the slaves just fight back?" Zelda thought to herself:

> They did fight back and the students need to know that. . . . Many organized through the network of the Underground Railroad itself, many organized within abolitionist movements, many slaves simply testified to life in the sheer act of survival and cultural preservation—but some slaves did revolt outright.

Her first impulse was to respond quickly to her student's question and provide some of this important information to open the discussion so students would understand slave resistance as part of the history of the time. But she hesitated before doing so wondering why this was not included in the curriculum in the first place. Was it because it was too violent? She noted that within this unit on slavery alone, her students would hear many stories of White violence. In fact, she wrote, "The entire context of slavery is violent by nature." It is important "to teach about violent histories" but to do so "in a developmentally appropriate way." Were there other reasons why slave resistance was not included that she was unaware of?

Zelda wanted to let both her Black students and her White students know that there was a strong history of Black resistance to slavery. At the same time she did not want to teach something too complex for her students to understand, or run the risk of having them leave the classroom "fearful or angry." Yet she could not let go of her own deep commitment to presenting history in a balanced way. She wrote:

> I feel that it is my responsibility within culturally responsive teaching to counter the "happy slave" archetype with source texts that provide for other, more culturally true archetypes, including that of the rebel. I feel it is my responsibility to answer such an important question.

To do otherwise, she explained, would be

telling a culturally biased story as if we somehow judge slave violence [to be] too rough for third graders to grapple with in the context of learning about slavery, an institution that is violent politically, economically, and culturally.

Zelda felt strongly that both the Black and White students should have the opportunity to grapple with the complexity of historical events. And they all deserved, as she said, "a right to have their people's stories told."

The Underground Railroad unit ended before Zelda had time to resolve her dilemma. Though she completed the unit, she was not done worrying about whether she let her students down by not responding directly to her student's question about why the Black people did not fight back. As the semester moved forward, Zelda found another opportunity to address her lingering concern. The class was about to read the last of the subject-specific biographies in their language arts unit. She added to the list of biographies the students would consider that of Nat Turner, who "led the best known of the American slave rebellions in 1831." She was relieved. At the same time, she knew this was just the first step in managing the larger dilemma of preparing an honest and balanced curriculum for her students while taking into account what was appropriate for 3rd graders and what her school required her to teach.

Whereas there are many dimensions to the urban school context that raise curricular dilemmas for teachers, the fact of racial, ethnic, and language diversity is one that is particularly poignant when it comes to making curricular and instructional choices. Diversity was the central issue in Karina's case, as it was in Zelda's. Diversity was the contextual factor salient in the majority of the curriculum dilemmas studied for this book, which is why I have chosen it as the focus of this curriculum chapter.

Some have argued that in recent years urban schools have become less rather than more diverse—that segregation has reconstituted itself in urban schools as White families flee the city, people of color remain unable to garner the resources to do the same, and immigrants flood in. But the student population of urban schools is still highly diverse, which means teachers must find ways to build a curriculum that addresses a wide range of student experiences, cultural backgrounds, and language differences. They must also trouble a curriculum that was constructed to reflect the lives, languages, and experiences of White Americans to reflect, instead, a population of students very few of whom are White.

Doing so is difficult, to say the least. Leora's dilemma provides a good example. Interestingly, it surfaced over teaching the same history content as Zelda but at the secondary level.

Leora's Dilemma

Leora teaches 11th-grade American History in a small school in the center of a large west coast city. She had a goal of finding ways to connect her many low-performing students with the content of her class. She was particularly concerned with the lack of engagement of two African American boys who appeared to have no interest in history, and no need to act as if they did. In spite of her efforts to take a culturally relevant approach to the material and make direct connections between the historical events they were studying and the students' current lives, she was not able to capture the attention of these two boys. This is where her dilemma began.

Her class was studying life in America's South at the time of slavery. Like Zelda, she had the idea that it was important to shed light on the strength of the African American population in this particular historical period by highlighting "methods of resilience and resistance in the African American experience of the 19th century (how enslaved peoples survived and thrived in this era of oppression)." Her plan had many goals. In addition to wanting to draw on historical events to show the human capacity for strength in the time of struggle, she wanted students to think deeply about the issues of this time period and how they are relevant today. She also wanted students to engage in the "doing of history" rather than only reading history as constructed by someone else.

She began by asking students to write in their journals their response to the Frederick Douglass quote "Without struggle there is no progress." Beginning with the words of an inspirational Black leader and focusing on means for changing one's life circumstances, Leora hoped to "push the students both academically and emotionally." Once students had written their own thoughts about Douglass's provocative quote and connected it to their own lives, she divided the students into two groups each of which was to prepare to debate about methods for social change: "One side was to argue that moral resilience was the superior method to end slavery and the other was to argue that physical resistance was the superior method." She provided students with "ten documents that [they] were to read and use in the ensuing debate to support their side." Her hope was that both

the topic of this investigation and the fact that it was they who were doing the investigating rather than the authors who wrote their textbook,
would draw her students in.

"The class got off to a good start," Leora reported. Students began
eagerly studying the documents, looking for evidence to support their ar-
guments for the upcoming debate. They were engaged, that is, except for
the two African American boys whose attention she had hoped to capture with this plan. Instead of working with their teammates, these two
separated themselves from their groups and took to fooling around with
one another, paying no attention to their groups' efforts. When Leora approached to try to get them on task one asked, "What this gotta do with
me? Why we gotta be bothered by this? It's stupid. We ain't no slaves, no
African peoples."

Their response distressed Leora. This lesson had everything to do
with them, she thought. They, and other young African American men,
are at the center of persistent struggle not only at their school but also
in the city where they live. Knowing how to study materials and frame
a debate based on evidence was a skill that could serve them well, as
would knowing how to plan for effective resistance. Beyond that Leora
hoped that learning the methods of collaborative inquiry with respect to
primary documents would be useful—to say nothing of the opportunity to
learn the American history they would need to know to pass the state's
exit exam. But most of all she was hoping they would see themselves in
the content of the lesson and identify with the strength and conviction of
their African and African American ancestors. From her pedagogy, which
included many opportunities to engage with both classmates and relevant
texts, she hoped they would recognize and develop skills that would help
them in both school and their lives outside of school. When none of this
worked as she had hoped it would she was left wondering, "Now what?"

The first thing Leora had to decide was how to respond to the resistance of these two students while attending to her other students who
were on board with the project and doing the work. She could not just
let these two continue to disengage—and yet forcing them to participate,
which she wasn't sure she could do anyway, would likely disrupt the work
of the others. Saddling the students who were enthusiastically preparing
for the debate with a teammate who did not want to be there didn't seem
like the right choice either. She also faced the larger dilemma of how to
reach these students in the long run to help them see the relevance of the
work of school for their futures. What would it take to convince these

boys that school could make a difference in their lives? Putting aside the fact of learning history, which Leora hoped she could convince her students was important, the harsh realities facing young Black men who drop out of school—unemployment, poverty, prison time, and even death—tormented Leora as she pondered what steps she could take.

Leora's case helps us see just how complex a professional challenge it is to create a culturally relevant and responsive curriculum. Whereas we can agree that teachers must connect their curriculum with the lives of their students, doing so is not easy. Leora's intention was good. She created a curricular and pedagogical plan that reflected the history of the students she wanted to bring on board as well as a pedagogical approach that required student engagement and relevant skill development. However, in the end the plan failed to engage the students for whom it was designed. In her analysis she raised a number of compelling questions: "What had happened that they did not see themselves in their heritage? Were they simply tired of hearing rhetoric from their teachers about equity and cultural pride?" She wondered about the students' ability to do the work and the literacy skills required of them to analyze the documents she provided, which led to her concern about her teaching and how much she had (or had not) prepared them for the task she asked them to do. She worried about her role in her students' disengagement and, once again, the reality of their "being left behind."

Leora's questions at the end of her narrative warrant our continued consideration when we think about preparing a curriculum that responds to the lives of the students we serve. She wondered if her students might perceive her curricular attempt, "as a moment of racism [during which] as a woman with White privilege I was to swoop in and teach these students about their culture when they themselves know worlds more than I ever will." She asked:

> When do discussion and discourse about cycles of oppression and social justice battles become benign rhetoric? At a certain level, when a student is thinking more about if (and how/what) he is going to eat for lunch next period, exploring slavery in depth doesn't seem pressing, but I guess the trick of the teaching trade is making those connections.

Leora, like many of her colleagues including Zelda and Karina who have chosen to teach in urban schools, continued to struggle to de-center her own experience as a White woman whose subject matter preparation focused on American history from a White perspective. Her goal was to develop a multicultural curriculum that was inclusive and held the promise of engaging her multicultural student population by offering them the opportunity to learn about their histories in the broader scope of their academic work. What it means to do that kind of meaningful curriculum planning, however, is not clear, as we can see in considering Leora's case. Choosing content that was informed by the words of a powerful Black leader, making it relevant to current issues in the Black community today, and employing a pedagogy that asked for genuine student input did not capture the attention or interest of the students for whom it was designed. We are left pondering with her, "Now what?"

RACE AND RACISM

Leora's question about her role as a White woman trying to teach in a culturally relevant manner surfaces race as a curricular factor in the urban school context in which racial and ethnic diversity are central characteristics. With race an additional factor comes into play—racism. For children of color who live in large cities with high levels of immigration and poverty, race and racism are matters of everyday life. Talking about race and struggling with racism are commonplace for most students in those settings. This is not so for many White teachers who, by virtue of their privilege, have struggled less with racism in their daily lives. Often they find the open expression of racial attitudes and racism unnerving. This is particularly so for novice teachers and, in particular, White novice teachers who are often the least familiar with and skilled at talking about race (Richert, Donahue, & LaBoskey, 2009; Tatum, 2007). Consider Rosella's dilemma as an example.

Rosella's Dilemma[1]

Rosella, a White woman, teaches a diverse group of 4th graders in a small middle-class school in an urban community. Among her goals was to provide students with a variety of texts in the different subject areas that represent the many ethnicities represented in her classroom. She began her unit on personal narratives by having students read from memoirs written by a diverse group of authors. Lucy, one of Rosella's White students, "took a shine" to the work of Maya Angelou and began reading her work enthusiastically. Soon after the project began Lucy asked Rosella if she had more examples of Angelou's work. Rosella was delighted and quickly sought out additional selections, being careful to select pieces that she thought were age appropriate.

Rosella's plan was to have the students consider how to write their own narratives after having had this opportunity to study the work of others. To begin this transition from reading to writing, she led a class discussion about what they had learned about the form of personal narrative from their exploration of the texts they had studied thus far. The class brainstormed this while Rosella noted their contributions on the board. To this list she added an insight of her own:

> The one I added to the list was that the experiences authors had affected their lives in profound ways. I gave the example that for Maya Angelou, growing up poor and Black in the segregated south helped shape the woman she would become.

This is where Rosella's dilemma began. The news that Maya Angelou was Black came as a shock to Lucy who immediately "burst out with an incredulous 'She's Black?! But she never said she was Black.'" Rosella wrote:

> I froze for a second and then replied, "Well, she never said she wasn't Black. . . . When you write a story do you start out by stating what your skin color is?" Lucy replied, "No, but that's different."

Rosella was at a loss for how to respond. She asked herself, "Why was that different? Why did Lucy assume the author was White unless told otherwise? Would a Black student have made the same assumption?" She had to say something but was uncertain where to begin. Should she begin a discussion about race—and if so, was she prepared to lead such a discussion? What about the work on personal narrative, she asked herself. Should she put that aside and deal with this question of race and identity first?

In Rosella's classroom race emerged as a curricular factor even though she had not planned for it in advance nor did she feel fully prepared to develop or enact this curriculum as she wished she had been able to do. She explained:

Before I could answer Lucy I had several decisions to make, the first one being, where did I want to take that class? The students clearly wanted to discuss the issue, but did I consider that an appropriate use of class time? The answer was and remains yes. I hope I will always consider social issues raised by my class to be of the utmost importance. The second decision had to do with figuring out where I as a teacher was comfortable in discussing race and finding ways to be comfortable when students' reactions or responses threw me. I wanted this discussion to be safe for everyone, but I had to feel secure with what we were discussing before I could effectively guide it. Was I prepared for that conversation? Not really . . .

Rosella's dilemma case is only one of several that describe class-room events where students raise questions of race that open a curricular opportunity to teach about it. In those moments, race as a topic can trump the planned curriculum. At the same time, many teachers feel unprepared to guide a discussion about race or do this curricular planning on the spot. As we think about such principles of teaching such as connecting the curriculum to the child, drawing on the students' funds of knowledge, and creating an embodied curriculum, we must keep in mind that we all are racial beings who will respond to the work of school in racialized ways.

Importantly, White students—and White teachers—are likely to raise issues of race only when theirs is not the story being told by the curriculum, as was the case Karina faced with her students in the dilem-ma narrative that opened this chapter (Howard, 1999; Lawrence, 1997; Tatum, 2007). Because the "grand narrative" of school subjects typically reflects a White perspective, White students are less disequilibrated by the lessons they encounter in school than the students of color who are their peers. As we make it safe for students of color to ask questions and offer different points of view, we must prepare ourselves for a curriculum that will grow in new ways. The descriptions of their classrooms described by the teachers whose work was studied for this volume make clear that race is a lens through which we view the world. As teachers we must not overlook the significance of race and must learn to open the conversation in our various subject areas to questions of race that will surely emerge.

Race is a factor that raises dilemmas for teachers in the classroom, as is racism, which also finds its way into the curriculum as students respond to what is being studied through the lens of their prior experiences. In some instances, the challenge for teachers comes not from the presence of different racial groups in school, which teachers can begin to address in the curriculum as we have seen in the work of Karina, Zelda, and Leora, but rather from the existence of racism in our society and the ways it plays out in the curriculum as well as the larger school context. Consider Omar, Jen's student, and his honest yet unanticipated contribution to the curriculum in Jen's classroom.

Jen's Dilemma

Jen, who is also White, teaches a newcomer class in a middle-school classroom in a community where she noted that there were "tensions between the Latino and the African American populations." The class was a language arts/social studies core class, which included language development activities for students new to the country and not yet proficient in English. Most students were 6th-graders, but there were 7th- and 8th-graders in the group as well. With the idea of creating a culturally relevant curriculum Jen decided to teach *The House on Mango Street* by Sandra Cisneros (1984). She reasoned that this would be an appropriate text for her class and one that they could connect with fairly easily since her students shared the immigrant experience with the book's characters and author.

To prepare her students for reading the book she assigned for homework several questions she believed would set the stage by connecting the life experiences of her students with the story they were about to read. She asked the students to "pretend that a friend is considering immigrating to the U.S. What are the good and bad things you would tell him or her about life here?" The following day the students shared their responses to the question in groups of four. As she walked around the room she observed the small groups talking and noted that the students had a lot to say to one another. Based on her observation she felt the curriculum was going well.

That night she took the students' papers home to read what they had said with the idea of continuing their conversation the next day. She planned to connect their thoughts and experiences recorded in their homework with those of Cisneros. The plan was a good one. For the most part the students' ideas were those she had anticipated—some good things about living in the United States and some bad: "good schools and the availability of jobs here on the positive side and violence, prejudice, and the dangers when crossing the border illegally on the negative." Omar's list of negatives was not one she had expected, however. It began with: "There are many African Americans here."

Omar's comment surprised Jen. He is a friendly, positive child who seemed to get along with everyone. She knew she needed to talk with him. Luckily she had the evening to think about how, but the extra time did little more than heighten her worry. Figuring out how to proceed was complicated by the fact that Omar had already shared his list earlier in the day with his small group. What was their response, she wondered, and how should she address Omar's comment with them? Perhaps she should start by talking with Omar directly. If she did, she wondered when that could happen and what she would say. She did not want to make him feel bad about himself or in any way isolate him from the group. If she proceeded by opening a discussion with the whole class about prejudice and where it comes from instead, perhaps Omar would see himself in the conversation and thus begin to question the fears and mistrust reflected in his homework list. She didn't want him to feel singled out and embarrassed, which he might, knowing that his group mates knew it was he who made a prejudiced comment on his homework sheet. In any case, Jen was grateful that she had assigned Cisneros's book. These short essays would be a good way to begin talking about this topic.

Whatever she decided to do regarding Omar's comment, the incident caused Jen to realize that the issue of race was an important one that warranted a place in her newcomers' curriculum. The more she thought about Omar, the more his feeling about African Americans made sense given the larger context of his life. Fear and mistrust based on race were alive and well in the diverse community where he and his classmates lived. There was considerable gang activity that influenced students' experience of race. The children were scared and so were their parents. The animosity between the African Americans who believed the Latinos had taken all their jobs and the Latinos who resented the cultural domination of the African Americans was considerable and not declining. It was likely that Omar's comment was a direct reflection of conversations he heard at home and in his neighborhood. Jen worried that if this building animosity were not addressed in school it was likely that her students would never have an opportunity to learn about racism in a monitored, guided, safe way.

Omar's answer to his homework assignment was an honest one. Perhaps by virtue of his age and experience in the United States he had not learned to mask his feelings and instead spoke from the heart. For this reason his contribution was a gift to Jen, and to those of us considering Jen's dilemma. While some might view Omar's response as racist, it does not necessarily reflect malice.. It is likely that Omar learned from the "curriculum" at home ways to defend himself in the face of the racism that is endemic in our society. As teachers we have the opportunity and the obligation to grapple with issues of race and racism in our classrooms. Whether we plan for this or not, both will become part of the urban school curriculum and teachers must be prepared to deal with them in constructive ways.

Jen's dilemma is one that is common in school settings where we ask students to connect the subject matters they are studying with their life experiences outside of school. Whereas the examples in the chapter have come from the language arts and social science curricular areas, issues of diversity and race extend beyond these areas. They pop up in math classes, science classes, physical education, art, and music. When we provide students with opportunities to speak from their own experience, and race and racism are part of their daily lives, we must be prepared for comments like Omar's and think through in advance how to respond. As members of a racist society, we and our students hold racist attitudes we are often unaware of. When these ideas appear spontaneously in the classroom discourse, the teacher is in the position of constructing a curricular response. To prepare for teaching about race and racism, teachers must come to new understandings of how race manifests itself in everyone's life. In so doing we can become smarter about the communities our students come from. Our work as teachers requires that we interrupt racism whenever it makes its way into our classrooms and schools. Learning how to do this is central to the work of teaching in urban—and all—schools.

CONCLUDING THOUGHTS

Part of what drives teachers like Karina, Leora, Zelda, Rosella, and Jen is the belief that schools can become institutions that bring about change in society by preparing all children with the knowledge and skills they need to participate as productive citizens. But doing that requires connecting the work of school with the life of the child. Broadening the curriculum to teach the "whole child"—that is, a curriculum that takes into account who the child is—is one aspect of accomplishing that goal. This idea is not new. Years ago Dewey (1902) wrote about the important connection between the curriculum and the child, arguing that they were at either end of the same continuum. He suggested that we abandon

> the notion of subject matter as something fixed and ready-made in itself, outside the child's experience; cease thinking of the child's experience as also something hard and fast; see it as something fluent, embryonic, vital; and [that] we realize that the child and the curriculum are simply two limits which define a single process.

The fact of diversity renders the task of connecting the curriculum with the child in this way extraordinarily complex. The dilemma examples we considered in this chapter suggest the types of curriculum dilemmas we might anticipate given the fact of diversity that characterizes most urban schools. One set of dilemmas concerns the challenges in developing and implementing a culturally relevant curriculum. Figuring out what will be culturally relevant when the cultures represented in any given classroom are broad and varied means that some students may feel left out (Karina's students, for example) and others feel erroneously included (Leora's students). Beyond considering broad cultural factors, such as ethnicity, in creating a curriculum, teachers need to have a deep understanding of the day-to-day cultural experiences of the students they teach. In this chapter we have focused on race and ethnicity as two examples of the kinds of diversity that present teachers with teaching dilemmas. Whereas these are two important kinds of diversity that exist in urban schools, they are only examples of the many ways children are different from one another. Responding to the diversity of one's students, while central to the work of teaching, predictably raises challenging dilemmas for teachers who aim to teach all children well.

What we might take away from our study of the dilemmas included here is that the curriculum of any classroom will necessarily reflect, not only what the teacher has planned, but also what the students bring with them to school. Recognizing the duality of these contributions of the teacher and the student—and anticipating the sometimes tense exchange between the two—will help teachers manage the dilemmas they will encounter as they work to create and implement a curricular and instructional plan that effectively meets the needs and aspirations of the widely diverse children and youth that populate our urban schools.

CHAPTER 5

What Have My Students Learned and How Will I Know?

Assessment Dilemmas

> I am struck by the responsibility of being a gatekeeper. I had
> the power to change his grade. I had the power to determine
> whether or not he deserved one more chance. I am still not sure
> I made the right decision, but I do know that he is not off the
> hook in my class. My expectations of him are higher and he still
> has another semester to pass. I realize that although I feel a
> tremendous anxiety about being a gatekeeper, Sam is also his
> own gatekeeper to a certain extent. So are his parents and his
> past experiences. For myself, I know that I would rather make the
> mistake of opening a door that should not be opened than closing
> a door that should stay open.
>
> Misha, *"The Gatekeeper"*

As we have seen in earlier dilemmas, part of assuming the title of "teacher" is recognizing the responsibility that comes along with the job. Nowhere in the work does this weigh more heavily than it does in assessing students. Misha's comment is from her reflection on a dilemma that concerned changing a student's grade. She was a high school science teacher. At the end of the term her student, Sam, who was taking Biology 1 for the second time, pleaded with her to add five percentage points to his grade to move it from an F to a D–. Misha had been working closely with Sam all year long. She met with him regularly, warning him frequently that he was in danger of failing her class. She wrote that he attended class regularly and presented no discipline problems. Although he seemed to try, he had trouble staying focused and had almost no follow-through on his assignments. Near the end of the semester he befriended students who were doing well in the class, which helped his grade a little, but his contribution to the work that was turned in remained questionable.

Just before grades were to be recorded Misha let the students see where they stood. When Sam saw his final grade he was upset and asked to speak with Misha privately after class. With a wavering voice and tear-filled eyes he said he would do anything for the 5% he needed to pass the course with a D–. She wrote, "He explained that if he got this F, any F this term, that he would be sent to job corps and not allowed to finish his schooling at Lincoln High." Over the next several days Misha agonized over this decision. In reviewing his science binder (which she asked for and received immediately) she found four assignments that he had completed that he had not turned in. If she counted these and let him do the extra curricular assignment that he had not yet done, he would have the points he needed. But she was conflicted about what she should do. She wondered about "the other five students who had failed the class, perhaps they had work that they had not turned in as well. Would changing his grade be fair to them?" She worried about her colleague teachers as well wondering what they would think of a decision to change a student's grade. Most difficult to her was what the impact of her decision would be on Sam. She was unclear about whether changing the grade would be "helping or hindering Sam's future and his ownership for his actions."

Weighing all the factors, in the end Misha decided to change Sam's grade and give him this additional chance. The experience left her shaken and uncertain that she had done the right thing. But in the end she decided that giving Sam this chance and having him succeed was a better option for her than "closing the door" and wondering later if for Sam this was a door that should have been left open.

Misha's dilemma opens our consideration of assessment, which some consider the most difficult of all teaching dilemmas. This is especially so when teachers encounter the many challenges involved in assessing students well, on the one hand, and the importance of doing so, on the other. Their role as evaluator requires that they make decisions that impact their students' lives in direct and consequential ways. While teachers are driven to be clear and fair in their assessments of student learning, once they encounter the realities and uncertainties of school life they begin to realize the complexities involved in accomplishing either. The assessment dilemmas in the pages that follow occur at this point of tension when teachers recognize what they want to accomplish in their assessment role, and what is possible given the many factors that impact their choices day to day.

LEARNING AND ASSESSMENT

We might begin our consideration of the assessment dilemmas by reviewing briefly the connection between learning and assessment to clarify how thoughtful assessment by teachers contributes to powerful student learning. Learning as presented in this text is a sociocultural phenomenon. In this view the students are active partners in the process, bringing with them diverse backgrounds and capabilities, requiring different approaches to curriculum, instruction, and assessment, all of which suggest how the assessment of student learning might occur (Vygotsky, 1978). Learning from a sociocultural perspective involves students and teachers learning together through a series of experiences that involve mutual engagement. This provides multiple opportunities for teachers to monitor what their students know and can do. It differs from the view that learning happens when the teacher tells students what she herself knows and then assesses her students to see if they remember what she has said.

From the sociocultural perspective assessment happens along the way as teachers view what their students know and are able to do. Sociocultural learning theorists explain that learning happens, not when students memorize what their teachers or their textbooks say, but when students participate with peers and their teachers in "communities of practice" to develop understanding and the ability to use knowledge flexibly in new and different ways (Vygotsky, 1978; Lave, 1996; Wenger, 1998). Through the various processes of teaching and learning together, the teacher is able to assess her students' accomplishments.

Assessment conceived in this way is formative and happens throughout the learning process, providing both the student and the teacher a sense of what the student knows and what needs to happen next so that knowledge will continue to grow. Opportunities for this kind of assessment are infrequent in schools where a form of summative evaluation prevails. Oakes and Lipton (2003) are helpful here in that they draw a distinction between assessment and evaluation. They define assessment as "gathering all the relevant information that can inform decisions about teaching, including information about the student and conditions for learning" (p. 244). The teacher's role is as ongoing collector of evidence of student learning. The understanding she develops as their work together goes along she then folds back into subsequent teaching decisions.

In contrast, Oakes and Lipton explain that "evaluation includes judgment of the student's performance and involves some element of whether the performance is *good*" (p. 244). The purpose is not only to judge students, but to sort them. The measure of goodness in this conceptualization reveals the normative nature of evaluation. What teachers contest is the standard for measuring "goodness" and whose decision it is to make that decision. In the current policy climate, the predominant standard of goodness is determined not locally, but rather at the district, state, and sometimes national levels. The school learning context—both its strengths and its challenges—are not accounted for in an evaluation scheme that relies on standardized tests as the key indicator of success. In addition to standardized tests, grades are an example of an evaluation mechanism that functions to judge and sort students. Grades, too, become problematic for teachers as we will see in the dilemma narratives included here.

ASSESSING STUDENT LEARNING IN URBAN SCHOOLS

Drawing on the Oakes and Lipton distinction we can see how powerful for student learning a well-conceived assessment plan would be. The approach would provide students multiple and ongoing opportunities to demonstrate what they know and, thus, provide teachers multiple ways of understanding what and how students learn. Assessing student learning in this way is difficult (some would argue impossible) to accomplish in the under-resourced urban setting. The prevalence of standardized tests is one reason. Currently teachers are required to gear instruction toward externally defined measures of student learning as the primary student outcome measure rather than toward ongoing, local, and individualized learning goals. Students who live in different cities, who come from different economic situations, who speak languages other than English at home, and whose prior school experience is not in this country are all tested on the same test at the same time. Given the purpose of comparing, judging, and sorting students, it is no surprise when a U.S.-born 3rd grader from a wealthy suburb outranks a peer from a poor urban district who has been in this country for less than 6 months and speaks only a modicum of English.

Typically students in poor communities score lower on the standardized tests than their middle- and upper-class peers. As a consequence they are subjected to more tests, based on the hope that monitoring their progress in this way will lead to eliminating the achievement gap. The result is that students who most need accurate assessments have fewer opportunities to demonstrate what they know and can do. Ironically, because of the time it takes to prepare for and take the tests, there is less instructional and learning time in their school lives as well. Often their teachers, in order to comply with the external mandates, find themselves acting in ways they believe are not in the best interest of their students.[1]

Sylvia provides an example. Her dilemma parallels Laura's, which we considered in Chapter 2. Laura's dilemma concerned her student Rosa who had to take a test in English without having the English proficiency the test required. For Sylvia, it was not only the inappropriateness of the test itself, but also the several month anticipation of it that caused her dilemma.

Sylvia's Dilemma

Sylvia teaches a grade 2/3 combination class in a large city. She titled her case "Welcome to America." She described the diversity of her 2nd and 3rd graders by highlighting not only their ethnic diversity but also their different learning challenges and other "special needs." She wrote,

> There are 13 boys and 8 girls, 17 second graders and 4 third graders
> . . . 9 Latino, 6 African American, 2 Bosnian, 1 Asian, 1 Pakistani,
> 1 Romanian, and 1 mixed. Three boys in the class are labeled as
> behavior problems, one of [whom] has recently been diagnosed with
> ADHD. There is also one boy with developmental delays and this
> is his first year in a mainstream class; last year he was in the Special
> Day Class at a different school in the District.

In addition to the diversity of her students, there was a constant flow of students in and out, common in many urban classrooms, adding complexity to the teaching challenges. "This is a classroom that has been constantly changing this year," Sylvia reported. "In the beginning of November, the school juggled students around in many of the classrooms and half of the students in my class were replaced with new students."

One of the many newcomers to her class in November was Randy, a recent immigrant. Randy arrived "directly from Romania," she reported. "This was his first school in the United States." He spoke not a word of English. Sylvia realized that teaching Randy would involve teaching him not only English and the 2nd-grade curriculum but also how to adjust to his new life in the United States. Having witnessed the adjustment struggle of her other class newcomers, she knew how hard it was to be in a new classroom in November when routines are already set and friendships have been formed. But for Randy who was not only new to the school but new to the country and the language as well, the hill to climb was enormously steep. It was equally steep for his teachers. Furthermore, the school did not have the resources to provide special help to Randy in his home language as it did for the Spanish-speaking majority.

Sylvia and her teaching partner developed an elaborate plan to help Randy. They had him working independently on his English and with partners in settings where he learned English and subject matter content at the same time. To all of this he responded well; he was eager to learn and cooperative, which helped him make slow but steady progress. Sylvia was able to assess his progress in a continuous way and use what she learned from these assessments to guide his subsequent learning. She explained:

> So, the rest of November and December was spent assessing Randy and constantly searching for resources to teach him English. After Winter Break, my partner teacher was able to create a buddy system with a couple of fourth grade students who came in and helped Randy with reading one-on-one . . . We also found computer interactive programs to help Randy with phonics and word study. These, and one-on-one work with either myself or my partner filled Randy's days. He began to progress and was able to carry on simple conversations in English with us. Randy was very cooperative, even though every day was a constant struggle for learning.

At the same time that things were progressing well for Randy, Sylvia became more and more anxious about the upcoming mandated California STAR (Standardized Testing and Reporting) tests scheduled for only a few months later. At the time, all 2nd graders were required to take these tests "whether or not they [spoke], read, or [wrote] English." Sylvia wondered how to handle the impending testing requirement. She questioned how Randy could take a test in English when he had so little command of the language and wondered what would be learned from his going through this demoralizing experience. Her understanding that these tests are designed to compare students with an externally determined standard and then again with his classmates fueled her concern. Forcing Randy to take the test felt like placing him in harm's way. However, since he had to take the test, Sylvia felt obligated to help him prepare as best she could. It was at this tension point that she faced her dilemma—should she move Randy from what he was doing to different work in an effort to help prepare him for the test or should she not interrupt Randy's steady progress and let the cards fall where they may when the test date arrived.

Ultimately, Sylvia decided to prepare Randy for the test by having him join in the test prep activities with his classmates. She and her partner teacher "began performing quick practice testing with the students to get them used to filling in bubbles and listening to questions" and included Randy when they did so. She explained,

> Second graders are not given test books with the questions in them; they have to listen to the questions and bubble in the answer they choose. Randy was included in these practices which were incredibly difficult for him. During the real testing, the teacher can only repeat a question twice—she cannot clarify the questions. Randy had to make whatever guesses he could.

In addition, Sylvia decided to bring Randy more into the activities of the class as a whole so that it wasn't only for test prep that he felt a part of the group. Previously he had spent much of his time working individually with one of his teachers, his 4th-grade buddy, and/or at the computer practicing his English skills. She reasoned that if she brought him into the fold more it would help prepare him for what was ahead. He would know more about tests and what his role would be in taking them.

But things did not work the way Sylvia hoped. Randy became "increasingly resistant and at times defiant." Even explaining to him why his classroom routines were interrupted was difficult. Sylvia wrote,

> I am unsure if he understands why this change has occurred. I have talked with Randy about it but from his expressions it is clear not everything was understood. This whole situation has me angry. How can STAR testing still be required in situations like these where the only result will be to label Randy as a below basic or far below basic student solely because of his lack of English proficiency?

Before the test prep began Randy was making good progress in this entirely new situation in which he found himself needing to learn not only English but also how to function in an American school classroom. The testing environment changed that for both Randy and also his teachers. Sylvia explained:

> Randy was a willing and eager student in the class until testing entered the picture. Now he has become angry, frustrated . . . This change had made it more difficult for Randy to progress in his

learning of English and more time is spent with the teachers working on behavior management with him, such as reminding him to stay seated in the chair and not to crawl under the table. The previous behaviors were not an issue when we worked with Randy at his rate of learning. It is because of standardized testing that Randy's routine has changed from a positive experience to a more negative one.

Sylvia's dilemma surfaced at the point of her considering whether and, if so, how to prepare Randy for the standardized test. It highlights the kind of challenge that standardized tests given in English raise for teachers in classrooms that serve populations of students who do not yet have the needed English proficiency.

Given the gift of hindsight, we might step back and consider what Sylvia's options were as she faced her dilemma. It was clear to her that Randy did not have the English proficiency to make sense of the test he was taking. Taking it would provide nothing more than she already knew about Randy's English proficiency and nothing more about Randy's understanding of the content the test was testing. One option she might have taken was to resist, which would be to have Randy not take the test at all but rather continue on with the instructional plan she and her partner teacher had put in place for him. Up until the point at which the test preparation work began, Randy was progressing well. Changing his routine only frustrated him and slowed down his progress. Whereas not taking the test might have been a better choice, as a new teacher, resisting in this way is difficult. It was hard to know if it is even possible to exempt a student from taking the test, and even more difficult to anticipate the consequences for Randy and others (including herself) if she chose that path.

Rather than acquiesce by just letting things fall as they might for Randy, which could have meant letting him alone and then having him take the test when the date arrived, Sylvia and her partner chose a path of accommodation. They tried to help him prepare for the test by moving him out of his specialized program to one that they hoped would help him feel less lost when the testing date arrived. This choice of accommodation is one that many teachers who have accepted standardized tests as a current-day reality are trying to balance with a plan that addresses student needs at the same time. If the tests are not going to disappear, then preparing students for them as best they can makes sense.

We have learned for close to a decade of doing this kind of accommodation, however, the high cost of this response in terms of instructional time and access to appropriate learning activities for students, in particular struggling students. We find ourselves questioning what beyond test taking skills our students are learning from the hours we spend preparing them for the tests. Randy's case was particularly poignant. It was clear that trying to prepare him for the test was not helpful. It appears that it may have been harmful, in fact. But for all of our students we must ask ourselves when faced with a dilemma such as the one Sylvia described, What in the end is in the best interest of the student or students we serve? Given our choices, what should we do?

TESTS AND OBJECTIVITY

Tests of various sorts have become the dominant assessment strategy in most public schools in the United States. Standardized tests are at the forefront and carry the highest stakes, but beyond those there are routine tests (spelling tests for example), teacher-made tests, textbook tests, unit tests, weekly tests, surprise tests, districtwide tests, and even intelligence tests. As the basis for evaluation, judgment, and sorting, some form of these tests makes its way into the classroom on a daily basis. Oakes and Lipton (2003) write, "Everybody wants a test to settle their concerns efficiently, scientifically, and fairly. Nearly every day each student is tested, results are reported, judgments are made and actions are taken" (p. 244).

Sylvia and Laura (Chapter 2) found themselves administering tests to students that were externally written and mandated by outsiders to the classroom work. In both cases, the tests were not aligned with either the curriculum being taught or the language level of the students taking the tests. The results therefore were meaningless in terms of assessing student performance in a way that could guide future teaching. The narrative dilemmas considered for this book included many examples of externally developed, mandated tests that were similarly disconnected from the curriculum and from the academic and/or language levels of the students. It is important to note, however, that even tests that are created by teachers do not necessarily solve the problem of misalignment between what is taught and what is tested. Consider Eunice.

Eunice's Dilemma

Eunice taught sophomore English in a large, diverse urban high school where the English classes are tracked. The higher two tracks required the students to write an essay for entrance. They also needed a 3.0 GPA (grade point average) and a successful interview with one of the English teachers. All the remaining students were in the lowest of the three tracks. It was in the lowest track that Eunice taught. She explained that because it was the "default" choice, the majority of the sophomores were in the lowest track where there was a wide variation in academic abilities, prior preparation, and languages spoken. In her class there were:

> eight English Language Learners, a handful of students previously in literacy intervention courses and students trying to earn high GPA's in order to get into AP or Honors English.

Eunice's dilemma came at the final assessment stage of a 9-week unit teaching Elie Wiesel's (1972) memoir, *Night*. She explained that though the text itself was short, the unit she and her partner teacher taught was long and elaborate and included "many supplemental readings, guest speakers, and even a field trip." The students were engaged, she reported, and worked hard. Not only did they seem to enjoy the book, but also "through the various assignments, discussions, and writings, it was evident . . . that they knew the content." Overall, she was pleased with what she and the students had accomplished, especially after hearing many stories from colleagues about how difficult it was to motivate "level three" students.

Her dilemma surfaced when she realized that unless she took a stand, the assessments she had gathered throughout the unit would potentially hold little weight in her final evaluation of their learning. While effective indicators of what this diverse group of students had learned during the 9-week unit, her partner teacher had previously written what she assumed would be the final test for the *Night* unit and was expecting all along to use the test as the final evaluation of the students' work. This test came as a surprise to Eunice. Up until the point of deciding how to grade their students she and her partner had co-planned the curriculum and made all decisions together. Eunice assumed that she would have an equal say in deciding how, in the end, students would be evaluated. This did not seem to be the case, which Eunice realized only as the unit was drawing to a close.

Eunice faced a dilemma. On the one hand, she felt she needed to honor her partner teacher's plan to give the test she had written and used in year's past. Her partner was the senior member of their team and believed fully in the test. That she had an answer key for the marking of results made her even more insistent about the value of the test because, she argued, it provided an "objective" measure of what the students had learned. Eunice, who read the test and found many of the questions ambiguous, felt the test was anything but objective. She wrote:

> As I tried to answer the questions on the multiple choice myself, I realized that many of them had multiple answers; but since the test was open book, I presumed that there had to be one answer that was "more" correct. When I approached my partner teacher nonchalantly about a few of the questions, she affirmed the correct answers with the teacher key. The multiple choice questions I struggled with asked students to think about the text figuratively and read beyond the literal meaning. The more I looked at the test and conferred with the book, I noticed there were many possible answers.

In writing the final test for the *Night* unit, Eunice's partner teacher set what she determined to be the standard against which the students would be measured. She assumed that the test grade would weigh heavily in determining the student's grade. Since Eunice did not know about the standard as reflected in this test, nor did she have any voice in establishing it, she did not teach toward it. Nor would she have had she known about the test (which again surfaces the "teaching to the test" phenomenon we considered earlier). Eunice did not feel that a multiple choice test was an appropriate way to measure her students' learning. In fact the use of a multiple choice test with questions that seemed ambiguous highlighted for her what she found problematic with these tests in general—the desire for efficiency at the expense of meaning. As a result, she did not feel it was fair to evaluate her students using it.

At the same time, knowing that she was the new and less experienced teacher, Eunice felt there was no getting around giving the test. Her dilemma shifted to how to incorporate the test results into her overall assessment of her students' learning. Her partner saw the test as the final summative assessment that demonstrated clearly what the students knew or did not know about *Night* and Elie Wiesel. Eunice felt the test provided little information about what the students had learned. Even considering it at all felt problematic to her. At the same time, since she had given the test and the students had spent time preparing for and taking it, she didn't feel she should ignore the results entirely either. Nor could she share her partner's deep belief in the test's ability to objectively measure the students' learning outcomes. At the time of her writing this narrative, she had not resolved her grading dilemma.

Eunice's situation of administering a test she had not had a hand in writing is not uncommon in schools. Being required to administer a particular test is not uncommon either. In the urban school setting such as Eunice's, where there is considerable pressure to raise grades and test scores on the one hand and high levels of diversity among the student population on the other, teachers' attention is consumed by many different matters. Eunice's focus was on the challenge of creating and implementing a curriculum and instructional plan that would meet her different students' learning needs. Given her understanding that students learn in different ways and at different rates, developing an assessment plan with multiple opportunities for students to demonstrate what they knew was essential as well. Since she and her partner had not talked about having a final test, and because she had built in several assessment opportunities for which she had rich data about what students knew, she was not worried about evaluating students as the unit drew to a close.

Eunice's dilemma raises the question of what the teacher's responsibility is—and ought to be—in assessing students according to externally determined standards. It is in this challenge that the standards movement and the push for standardized tests are both located. The question we face as teachers is how to establish high standards for all students and then measure their and our success in meeting those standards. Whereas establishing high standards for all students is an important equity issue, how to and who should define those standards as well as how to measure how well students meet them are questions that are still unanswered.

This dilemma raises the question of objectivity in testing as well. One reason the testing movement has garnered such momentum in the United States is the goal of objectivity. Tests that are properly constructed employ a technology designed to ensure reliability, validity, and trustworthiness (Oakes & Lipton, 2003, p. 245). Objectivity is the intended outcome of this test construction technology. The idea of tests being an objective measure of what students know carries over in many instances to even nonstandardized tests, such as the one Eunice gave her students. Eunice's case reveals the fallacy of this notion. Objectivity requires that the test questions are not open to interpretation or dispute. We see that this was not the case for Eunice's test. Many argue that, ultimately, objectivity is not possible in even more "scientifically" constructed test situations, which are posited as both "valid" and "reliable." The quest for objectivity in assessing students in the uncertain, diverse, and changing world of schools is a goal in education that keeps teachers awake long into the night.

SUBJECTIVE FACTORS AND GRADING

Many teachers feel paralyzed by wanting to be "objective" in their evaluation of their students' performance, recognizing that their assessments cannot easily overlook the subjective factors that impact students' work. In the urban setting, as in all settings, these factors are numerous. We can begin to predict what they will be for children in urban schools given characteristics of the setting we have already discussed such as high levels of poverty, a broad range of cultural differences and associated learning processes, language diversity, violence in the community, and under-resourced schools that have not prepared children well for the academic work ahead. Whereas most teachers wish they could find some purely objective way to evaluate students, the reality is that subjective factors impacting school performance must be accounted for when evaluating students as well. Consider Luella's struggle to evaluate the work of her student Juanita.

Luella's Dilemma

In Luella's high school Intermediate Algebra class there were fifteen 11th- and 12th-graders, all of whom were struggling to learn math. Two of the fifteen were engaged in this struggle as second language learners. While the other students in the class spoke English as their first language, Luella explained they had "never achieved proficiency in basic math skills such as fractions, decimals, or percents." Most had "just barely" managed to pass Algebra 1 and Geometry. Luella's challenge was to work with this group on basic math skills and get them ready for taking Algebra 2.

Luella's dilemma focuses on how to evaluate one of her two ELL students, Juanita. Juanita was a good student in many ways. She "[came] on time every day," which was not something that was true for most of her classmates. In class she "[was] well behaved and never [failed] to turn in all of her homework on time." Though she worked extremely hard and appeared to be understanding the math as the lessons moved along, Luella found when Juanita worked with her one-on-one there were significant underlying misconceptions that consistently got in the way of her learning. With Luella's help Juanita was able to get back on track—or at least to appear to be back on track. But her test results indicated that she didn't stay on track for long:

> When I monitor her during class work, I am generally able to catch her errors and put her back on the right track. Her class work is fine, and her homework is okay. Her tests, however, are a whole different story. Unlike her homework and her class work, her tests are an absolute disaster. Out of 40 possible points she'll typically score 15. They seem to indicate that she has learned very little.

Why Juanita did so poorly on tests is unclear. Luella believed it was because she didn't understand the math, which was probably the case. However there could be other reasons Juanita struggled with tests. Luella felt there could be a language barrier getting in the way or possibly test anxiety. Whatever the reason, Juanita's test performance was poor and Luella was left with the dilemma of having to give her a grade that signified what she had learned and what she knew of the math curriculum. The tests were designed to provide her the information she needed to make that determination.

Luella's narrative is important for our consideration of assessment dilemmas because it opens the door for considering the two uses of tests: one for the summative work of grading and evaluation that function to judge and sort students and, two, for the formative work of identifying strengths and challenges learners face to guide future teaching and learning. Luella's struggle revealed the problem with using tests as the primary, summative, and often single tool for grading students. When tests are used instead in a formative way they can be a mechanism for indicating student misconceptions and thus provide a starting point for addressing student learning needs.

Luella could have used Juanita's incorrect test answers to focus the interventions she used to help her learn if she were not using the test to grade Juanita but, rather, to assess what Juanita understood and did not understand. She could have asked Juanita to show her how she arrived at her answer, for example, which would guide Luella's teaching toward addressing whatever stumbling blocks seemed to be in the way. Used in this way the test could also have been a tool for Juanita as it would have provided her feedback on what she still needed to learn. Rather than something to be dreaded and feared, the test used in a formative way could have become a mechanism that Juanita saw as an enhancement for helping her learn. If test anxiety (or math anxiety) were at partial fault for Juanita's poor test performance, using tests in this formative manner would have begun to address that problem as well.

Sadly, as described by Luella, the intention of the test in this instance was for grading and therefore functioned in a summative rather than formative way. For Juanita the test might have captured what she knew—though because of the potential language barrier, we cannot be sure. As the only factor in her grade, however, the test left out of the picture other factors that were important to Luella as well. Her dilemma came in determining Juanita's grade.

Luella's uncertainty surfaces the question of objectivity in student grading that we began to consider with Eunice's case. In addition to the more objective measures of what math content Juanita knew, were subjective factors that Luella wanted to acknowledge. She wrote, "I am torn between giving [Juanita] a C or a D, especially when her tests are mostly Fs." A grade of C didn't accurately reflect what Juanita knew. On the other hand, a D didn't reflect her work in the class either. Luella believed her effort in class, her perfect attendance, and her continued engagement all warranted acknowledgment in Juanita's grade.

Luella's reasoning through her dilemma about grading Juanita reveals how complex this decision was. Part of this difficulty came in anticipating how Juanita would react when she saw how Luella judged her performance. She wanted Juanita's grade to reflect her hard work and commitment to learning, but giving her a higher grade than she had earned communicated an inaccurate judgment of what she actually knew about the math content. Luella knew that whatever grade she gave would impact Juanita.

> My dilemma is that if I give her the grade that is somewhat better than her learning indicates I might be doing her a disservice because it may lead her to believe she understands more than she actually does. She may move on to Algebra 2 without knowing enough to be successful.

We notice here that Luella seemed to believe that Juanita's test scores were accurate indicators of what she knew of the course's math content, which we realize may or may not have been true. At the same time Luella worried that giving Juanita the lower grade that reflected only how she performed on the tests and nothing more might have discouraged her. "She might possibly learn that all the effort she puts forth will not amount to anything. . . . I want her to keep trying and to keep coming on time, to keep doing her homework and not to give up," Luella wrote.

Luella's struggle to determine Juanita's grade is an example of a phenomenon experienced by all teachers, not just those in urban schools. Knowing what grades to give is never easy. But Luella's case points our attention to several details of the urban context in particular that are relevant to understanding the assessment dilemmas faced by teachers in this setting. As we have seen in all of the cases we've considered thus far in this chapter, urban schools typically have large numbers of immigrant students, many of whom don't speak English as their first language. In fact, having only two English Language Learners in Luella's class is an uncharacteristically low percentage given her school's location in a large urban center. Working with English Language Learners places the teacher in a difficult spot when it comes to evaluating student work and determining grades. Luella wonders how much of Juanita's difficulty in math comes from her not understanding English fully. What role does language have in the summative evaluation of student work? What role should it have if we are concerned with equity and social justice?

A related question concerns Juanita's prior learning and how prepared she was in math before coming to the United States. If she had gone to elementary and middle school in Mexico, for example, we might wonder what mathematics she learned there and how closely that aligned with what was taught in California where Juanita was now in school. If Juanita were American born with all of her prior schooling in the United States, her prior math background might also have been compromised if those experiences were in poor under-resourced schools where the math teacher was not certified in math. All of these could be factors relevant to the situation Luella described.

Luella's case raises the matter of the subjective nature of grading and evaluation. It harkens back to our earlier discussion of the importance of knowing students well in order to teach them well. Knowing what they know, what they care about, what their prior schooling experiences were, what languages they speak, what learning traditions they bring with them from their homes, and so forth, are all helpful to teachers trying to create a culturally responsive curriculum. While knowing about a student's life enhances one's ability to teach them, it may also diminish one's ability to assess them. This is particularly true when part of what we know about a student's life—conditions such as poverty or violence—dominate our concern for their well-being. Challenges such as these impact student learning and school performance and for many teachers render difficult the processes involved in assessing them. Tanya's case provides a compelling example.

Tanya's Dilemma

Tanya is a 12th-grade English teacher at a small public school in a poor neighborhood in a large west coast city. To raise academic performance at the site, the faculty had developed a project-based learning program guided by detailed rubrics outlining performance standards and associated habits of mind. Each class had several "certification assignments," which students needed to complete and pass in order to graduate. At the outset of her teaching assignment Tanya agreed to follow her partner teacher's "no late work" policy. Since one of the goals the school held for its students was responsibility for one's actions, turning work in on time seemed like one way to teach and assess for that outcome. It turned out that, while turning work in on time was a reasonable criterion for assessment, as it was for Luella's student Juanita, for other students the criterion might not have made as much sense. This was the situation for Miriam, Tanya's student whose life circumstances rendered difficult the strict adherence to the class's assignment calendar.

Miriam was one of 26 students in Tanya's diverse English class. Sixteen of the 26 students were Latino, three were Black, two were Arab, and five were Southeast Asian. "Seven are designated as English Language learners and thirteen are redesignated English learners." None of the 26 is proficient in academic English. Nor have they developed good study skills, which accounts for the strict policies governing assignments, no late work, and other similar "organization" skill requirements. Tanya explained:

Nearly all of the students have very poor organization and study skills. They rarely complete homework assignments and struggle to manage their time effectively. To accommodate this problem, my partner teacher and I emphasize class work over homework and provide some in-class time for students to work on major assignments.

Miriam was an 18-year-old Mexican American young mother of a 2-year old daughter, Nancy. Nancy's father was a senior at the school, though he was not in Tanya's class. Tanya explained that Miriam's mother takes care of Nancy during the school day, but after school Miriam takes on all the child care responsibilities. As far as Tanya observed, Nancy's father is not involved in the child care at all.

Miriam told Tanya that being a mom motivated her to be a good student. She wanted to be a good role model for her daughter, and she had the potential to be one. She was a capable student academically though not one who could easily meet the strict class-performance guidelines, Tanya explained. She was absent frequently and struggled to turn work in on time. In spite of this, Miriam possessed "some of the strongest reading and writing skills in the class, and in the first marking period of the semester she received a B+ in English." It was the tension between Miriam's strengths as a student and the nonschool demands on her that took her attention away from being one. This was at the heart of Tanya's assessment dilemma.

As the culminating assignment for her class unit studying the memoir *When Heaven and Earth Changed Places* (Hayslip and Wurts, 2003), students were to write an essay analyzing the book's theme. "Because this is a certification assignment," Tanya wrote,

> Students must receive at least a C– on the essay in order to pass English and graduate from high school. If a student fails the assignment s/he is required to revise the essay for a higher grade.

Tanya extended the deadline for the essay several times due to a number of school schedule changes including a senior field trip that she did not know about in advance and, subsequently, an impromptu college visit trip scheduled by the counseling office. Even with those changes, several students requested a further extension, including Miriam, who "explained that Nancy had come down with a cold . . . and she had been busy and distracted caring for her." Tanya granted all of the extension requests, including Miriam's.

When the day came for Miriam to turn in her essay, she contacted Tanya to tell her she had not finished it but would send it in by midnight thus making the due date deadline. However, midnight came and went with no essay from Miriam. The following morning Tanya received an email from Miriam indicating that her essay was not done. In her note she explained that though she tried to finish the essay she had "too much in (her) head and too many things to worry about" and she couldn't get it done. Though she knew that her grade would be impacted, she held out hope that Tanya would still accept the paper. Miriam wrote, "I also understand if you think you have given us enough time to finish it and if you do not want to take my essay its fine. I mean no its not but I'll take that."

The email presented Tanya with the next in this collection of dilemmas associated with assessing Miriam's work. She wrote:

> When I received Miriam's 2:00 AM email I was very uncertain about what action to take. I had been very clear in Friday's class that the absolute final deadline was Friday night at midnight and I did not want to give any students the impression that my "final" word was subject to change. However, I wanted to accommodate Miriam's challenging responsibilities as a parent, and I was also impressed that Miriam had proactively contacted me to explain her circumstances. Furthermore, I was worried that if I refused Miriam's request, she would fail to turn in the essay at all and would thus be ineligible for graduation.

Tanya responded to Miriam's email indicating that she could turn in the essay over the weekend giving her several more days. But the weekend passed and the essay did not arrive. When it did arrive, more than a week later, Tanya again had to decide what she should do in terms of Miriam's grade. Miriam's essay was excellent and worthy of an A as measured by the grading rubric. However, it arrived way past the deadline in a grading system designed to teach academic responsibility as well as academic skill development. Tanya was torn. Unlike the other students in the class, Miriam was a mom with many demands and pressures at home. It is understandable that an essay deadline may end up lower on the list of priorities for an 18-year-old mother trying to make her way in the world.

Tanya's dilemma is an important one for our collection because it moves us away from thinking that all assessment dilemmas are connected with tests—and standardized tests in particular. This is far from the truth. Ultimately, the dilemmas associated with assessing student learning come in determining what the assessment should—and does—measure, as well as the consequences of those assessments for the students. We saw how Luella struggled with the consequences of giving Juanita a grade that would not discourage her from continuing in math, but would also communicate as best she could the level of Juanita's math skills. Tanya struggled as well with what for Miriam would be the consequences of her grade. If the purpose of the assessment were solely to grade students, then the teacher would be caught needing to carefully weigh the consequences of awarding the grade against the broader purposes of her teaching.

What is difficult for teachers is that they seldom have only one purpose guiding their work. The assessment process often pits one purpose held dear to the teacher, and to society, against another that is equally important. This is what occurred for Tanya. Tanya saw teaching the skills of essay writing as an important goal of hers as an English teacher. One strategy she had for teaching those skills to Miriam and her classmates was to create a rubric that set out the components of a good essay. She directed her students to use the rubric as a guide for their final writing assignment. Tanya's purpose for teaching, her teaching, and her assessment plan were well aligned. Miriam's work demonstrated that Tanya had accomplished her goal. "Miriam's essay was excellent," Tanya wrote. "She received a solid A according to the rubric, and she wrote one of the best essays in the class."

If Tanya's only goal in teaching Miriam had been to prepare her to write an essay, there would not have been a problem. However, Tanya held a competing goal for Miriam: She wanted to help her develop her organizational skills, including honoring deadlines. The assessment criterion for this was the student turns work in on time. Miriam did less well in meeting this standard, although her reasons for falling short of this standard were easy to understand. She consistently turned work in late, including the final essay, which came in weeks late in spite of several extensions.

As the semester came to a close, Tanya was left needing to weigh these two important goals against one another, and determine which of the two would carry more weight in determining Miriam's final grade. Since she had agreed with her partner teacher at the outset of the semester to a "no late work" policy, she felt she should give "Miriam a zero on this high-quality essay because it was turned in late." The decision was extremely difficult for Tanya. She knew it was important to help her students "become more successful at navigating academic and professional worlds," which she felt "requires them to meet important deadlines." At the same time Miriam had done good work, which also deserved recognition. That Miriam was juggling her parental responsibilities with her schoolwork made Tanya "want to accommodate her uniquely demanding circumstances" as well.

In Tanya's case, as well as the other cases we have considered thus far, there were contextual factors that contributed to the complexity of Tanya's dilemma and to the predictability of such dilemmas for the urban teacher. For Tanya, the circumstance had to do with the challenges her student faced managing the responsibilities of being a mother with those of being a student. Teenage parenting is a factor in high schools, in general, and urban schools in particular.

As Miriam's teacher, Tanya had to balance her understanding of pressures on Miriam with the academic goals she held for her. It was clear to Tanya that Miriam's writing skills were developing well. As an English teacher, this was highest on her list of concerns. At the same time, she had agreed to support the schools goal of teaching responsibility as a second central purpose of her course, which meant that she also had to consider this in determining Miriam's grade. Ultimately her two important and somewhat competing goals along with the circumstances of Miriam's life and experiences outside of school merged in the form of a gripping dilemma. When the semester drew to a close, Tanya found herself facing the inevitable task of assigning Miriam a grade. At the time of sharing her dilemma narrative, she had not yet done so, which leaves us uncertain about what she did and wondering what we would do in her shoes. Thinking along side Tanya makes painfully clear just how challenging, complicated, and even agonizing the process of deciding "what to do" can be.

CONCLUDING THOUGHTS

Miriam's dilemma provides an additional example of how assessing student learning and performance raises questions for teachers: Are my assessment criteria clear? Are they fair? Do they measure what I taught? Do students have adequate information to study for the test? Are there multiple ways students can demonstrate what they know? These questions frame dilemmas about how to assess students in ways that support their learning. As student understanding is made visible by a well-planned assessment system, both the teacher and her students have a way of knowing what students are learning and what they are not. They can also begin to tell *how* students are learning and what challenges students face as they do so. The information gleaned from such an incremental assessment system allows the teacher to tailor future instruction to meet student needs. The potential for academic success rises accordingly.

As we have seen in the cases reviewed in this chapter, the urban context further complicates an already complicated and challenging process. Teachers find themselves wondering about the additional stresses faced by students taking tests in English when they lack proficiency in English, or by students whose life circumstances are stressed by responsibilities outside of school. A teenage mother has much to manage in addition to her schoolwork. A child recently arrived from Eastern Europe must spend time learning the ways of American schools in addition to English and whatever content he is expected to learn. The stresses associated with language proficiency, family responsibilities, poverty, and immigration challenges all affect students' abilities to perform well on externally developed, standardized measures. Teachers teaching children whose lives are influenced by those factors find themselves struggling with assessment dilemmas everyday.

And yet assessing student learning is central to good teaching. It is the role and responsibility of the teacher to set high standards for all students and to help them reach those standards. Assessing their work along the way of a carefully designed curriculum and instructional plan helps students learn what they are doing well and what will require additional work. If assessments are used to help students monitor their learning rather than as a punitive measure used to judge what they don't know, students can come to understand that learning is possible. Many students hold the belief that they are not smart—that intelligence is an inborn immutable trait that they do or do not have. This belief is reinforced by an assessment program that tells them over and over again that they are "below proficient" or worse. With an assessment system that helps students monitor their progress toward an explicit and well-understood goal, they can come to see that they can become smart with the help of a teacher who guides their progress in an intentional way. All students must be held to high standards. A well-conceived and executed assessment system is a key factor in helping students get there. It is an indicator of a teacher's belief in the capacity of all children to learn.

In the assessment system as we know it currently, evaluation and grades are mechanisms for sorting students. Students who begin the "race to the top" without the prerequisite knowledge and/or English language skills to compete are undoubtedly going to end up falling to the bottom.

For all of the students in the cases discussed here, who are trying to learn, the consequences can be devastating. The dilemma for teachers involves knowing how important assessment is to guide their instruction. Keeping track of what students understand and can do is essential for teachers as they decide next steps in the teaching of those students.

Assessment seen in this way is an important component of curriculum development aimed at equity and social justice. As teachers learn to manage the assessment dilemmas they will predictably face in their urban school settings, they must hold onto the high standards they have for the students they serve and must plan a curriculum that includes an assessment system to help students accomplish those goals. They must also keep in mind what is most important to them and be prepared to prioritize values that will compete with one another as they make difficult assessment decisions. The work of assessing students learning is daunting, but anticipating the challenges in advance can help us align our teaching decisions with the goals we hold for the children and communities we serve.

CHAPTER 6

What Will I Do?

The hardest choices are not between what's right and what's wrong, but what's right and what's best.

Ford, 2009, p. 204

The centerpiece of Jamie Ford's (2009) novel *Hotel on the Corner of Bitter and Sweet* is the tense relationship between Henry, an American-born Chinese adolescent and his Chinese-born father. Lessons about life and how to live it, such as this one from Henry's dad about how to act when the path is not easy or obvious often burden Henry, who wants the freedom to live in the way he sees his peers living—less controlled by their fathers and able to make decisions about what they intend to do on their own. Yet sometimes Henry's father's lessons inspire him. His father's challenge to recognize the consequences of his decisions and weigh them before acting was one of those ideas Henry found inspiring. How should he act when asked by his teachers or his peers to do things he deems questionable or unreasonable? What does it mean to choose what's "best"—and best for whom? If something seems "right" according to the school rules, yet clearly hurtful to people he cares about, what should he do?

The criteria of "right" and "best" for decision making are those we have used as we pondered the dilemma cases shared with us by the novice teachers highlighted in this book. Tanya's dilemma, which we considered at the close of Chapter 5, provides a good example. Tanya had to decide how to grade Miriam, her student who was a teenage mother with a two-year-old daughter. If only the decision had been to decide between right and wrong. Instead, Tanya had to choose between what she believed was right according to school policy and what she considered best for Miriam. The many factors she needed to consider included the promise she made when taking her job that her grades would account for students meeting deadlines. Her school identified "responsibility" high on its list of school goals. The teachers agreed that if an important assignment comes in late, the student would receive an automatic "F."

It was true that Miriam's work was consistently turned in late; there was no getting around that. She knew the rules and the consequences. Given that, Tanya considered perhaps what was right was to grade her accordingly, which would mean failing her. But would this be best for Miriam? She doubted it would. Then again, she didn't know for sure. Tanya did know that Miriam's responsibilities as a teenage mother sometimes made it impossible to turn in her work on schedule. She knew also that Miriam was serious about her studies and she was a good student in many ways, one of the best in her class. Like her colleague teachers whose cases we studied in this book, Tanya found herself on the horns of a dilemma. And as Henry's father predicted, the hardest part of her decision about how to act was to choose between what she considered "right" and what was "best."

THE MORAL ASPECT OF TEACHERS' PROFESSIONAL RESPONSIBILITY

Choosing what's best for one's students is not only a professional responsibility of teaching but a moral one as well. The decisions teachers make have consequences that impact their students' lives. Though they strive to make their decisions based on what they believe will be in their students' best interest, it is seldom clear what that best interest would be especially since judging the consequences in advance of the action is difficult. The moral aspect of this decision-making process is attached to this uncertainty. It places teachers in the position of making decisions for action based, not only on what they know about the student and the situation including the school rules and procedures, but also on what they value and believe. To complicate things further, the values that guide teachers and that they hold dear often compete with one another, rendering the decision process more difficult still.

Let us consider Tanya's dilemma one more time. Tanya knows that managing the Miriam-grade dilemma involves considering both the larger purposes of her teaching (why she is teaching in the first place and what she hopes to accomplish with her students) and the consequences of any decision she decides to make for Miriam and for everyone else involved. She reasons that if she makes an exception to the grading rule for Miriam and passes her in spite of the clearly defined and published rules of the school regarding late work, there would be consequences not only for Miriam but also for the other students in her class. With fairness as a moral principle she holds in high regard, Tanya struggled wondering how fair (or unfair) it would be to pass Miriam and not her classmates who also turned in late work. What would such a decision communicate to them? Miriam's situation is clearly unique and warrants special consideration. The particular challenge of raising a child at the same time as being a high school student put her in a special category. But what about the circumstances facing the other students in the class? Perhaps they, too, faced obstacles that she did not know about that would put them in some kind of special category as well.

While Tanya wanted to be fair and she valued fairness as a guiding principle, she also wanted to be caring, which turned out to be a competing value in determining her grading decision. She asked herself if it was caring to hold Miriam back when she clearly could do the work. She knew Miriam was a good student who in spite of the challenges had accomplished the learning goals for writing that she had set for her. Miriam was also tenacious—a characteristic Tanya valued and admired. Would it be caring to not acknowledge her effort and what she was able to accomplish as an outcome? Given there was no clear right and wrong action for Tanya to take in grading Miriam, she had to rely on her judgment—informed by her values and beliefs as much as her knowledge—to make her decision. She knew she was not only professionally responsible for doing so but morally responsible as well.

A COMMITMENT TO ACT

The imperative at the end of this sometimes-painful deliberation that teachers go through is that they must act. Taking that step can be emotionally fraught because the action typically involves a compromise of some part of what the teacher believes and values. Compromises become a predictable part of what the work requires, as does knowing that one must act even without certainty of the consequences of that action. The combination of these factors makes the decision-making process and subsequent action all the more challenging. Acting under these circumstances takes courage.

We have said repeatedly in this book that teaching is uncertain work. Functioning in a context where questions about what to do abound, creates the need for both professional and moral judgment on the part of the teacher. Teachers are bound by professional standards to reason through the dilemmas that face them and act in ways that they believe will be best for their students. And while they can't be sure of the consequences of their choices, that they make choices and act is imperative.

As we look back at the dilemmas we pondered over these chapters, we can see how the process of managing dilemmas unfolds. It begins with the teacher recognizing that the situation she faces is a dilemma rather than a problem with an easy solution. She frames the dilemma by considering both her purposes for any particular action and the consequences of any action she might take. The question "What should I do?" is followed by "What can I do?" which acknowledges the constraints teachers face in making decisions. In spite of those constraints (institutional rules and regulations, community customs, school norms, etc.) and coupled with the indeterminate nature of the outcomes, ultimately the teacher must ask and answer the question "What will I do?" Then she must find the courage to act.

Learning from Our Actions

The commitment to act in a professionally and morally responsible way does not end with the action, however. The action is followed by reflection on the action, which creates the next stage of learning for the teacher in this dilemma-management process. By reflecting on our decisions and the actions we take as a result we can begin to build our understanding of what actions result in what outcomes. Reflection offers the opportunity to build our base of professional knowledge and our confidence as professionals at the same time. Putting our own professional learning at the heart of our teaching is an important piece of the moral imperative of our work as teachers. It reflects a commitment to meeting students' needs. And even though we can't be certain of the consequences the next time we encounter a similar set of circumstances, having reflected on our decisions and actions we will be closer in our assessments of what "works" for students and what does not. Learning by reflecting on our work allows us to change what we do as the students and the circumstances surrounding those students change over time.

Assuming an Inquiry Stance

Reflecting on our actions in this way privileges experience as a source of knowledge for teachers. In fact, we often hear in the profession that most of what teachers know, they learn from experience. We must keep in mind that having an experience is different from learning from experience. To learn from our experiences we must take the time to think about them and make sense of the action outcomes. Teachers who approach their teaching with an inquiry stance are accustomed to asking questions that connect their actions with the consequences for their students. In managing the dilemmas of practice they will ask such questions as What happened as a result of my action? What were the unanticipated consequences? Did the consequences I observe line up with my purpose? If so, how and if not, why not? Given what I know now what will I do the next time I encounter a situation like this? What can I learn from this experience about acting in the best interest of my students? These questions and others like them launch a learning path for teachers. They are evidence of the teachers' professional and moral commitment to do right by the students they serve.

MITIGATING THE UNCERTAINTY OF TEACHING

Whereas teaching is uncertain work, the dilemma cases presented here are offered as a way to mitigate some of that uncertainty. They do this in a number of ways. To start, just recognizing the difference between a teaching problem that can be solved and a dilemma that must be managed can begin to mitigate teaching's uncertain nature. Without making this important distinction teachers find themselves agonizing over dilemmas searching for the "right" answer about how to act when, in fact, there is no right answer to be found. If teachers can sort through and separate problems from the dilemmas, they will have accomplished the first step in managing them both. Knowing that dilemmas do not have easy, foolproof, "right," answers can help teachers begin the process described above of considering possible ways to respond to their students' needs and line those needs up with their purposes and the possible consequences of any action they might take.

   Recognizing that however difficult the dilemmas of practice might be, they are also predictable, which offers a second way of mitigating the inherent uncertainty of teaching. Schwab's (1983) commonplace categories of teacher, student, and content (which for the purposes of this book includes curriculum, instruction, and assessment) suggest one possible set of categories of dilemmas that are likely to hook teachers. Within the category of teacher we considered dilemmas concerning professional identity. All teachers can anticipate that they will face questions of identity and authority in their practice. Coming to see oneself as the person in charge, or the authority in the classroom is challenging and remains challenging for many teachers throughout their careers. Situations that test one's authority and confidence as a teacher, such as those we considered in Chapter 2, that come from students or parents, (or outsiders such as those who mandate standardized tests) will predictably stump teachers who have a need to be in control, on the one hand, but want to take into account the opinions of others, on the other. Talking with colleagues about the challenges of easing into their new professional role by sharing their dilemmas, as the teachers who offered their cases for our consideration have done in this text, can help teachers undo some of the uncertainty they will undoubtedly feel as they define and redefine themselves as teachers over the span of their careers.

The second category of predictable dilemmas we considered was that of students, in which we considered dilemmas concerning care and student-teacher relationships. We reasoned that to teach students well teachers must know them well. But coming to know one's students can be difficult. For teachers in urban schools the process often involves crossing race, language, and/or class lines. Knowing how to do this in ways that are culturally appropriate can be challenging and likely to present dilemmas such as those we examined in Chapter 3.

Once a teacher knows about the life of the student outside of school, she or he must then figure out if and how that knowledge should impact the work with that student in the school context. This is another area of predictable dilemmas in the student category that teachers can anticipate. Knowing that Miriam has a 2-year old child, for example, was important for Tanya's understanding of her work in Tanya's classroom (Chapter 5). But knowing how to account for that in grading her left Tanya perplexed. Knowing that Cameron's sister was soon to be released from jail was important to Emily's work (Chapter 3) but left her uncertain when she learned he wanted to get a gun so he could protect her. Considering the student dilemmas presented here is a starting place for thinking about the challenges that will predictably face teachers and in this way begin the dilemma management process.

Drawing on Schwab's (1983) category of content, we reasoned through dilemmas having to do with creating, enacting, and assessing a curriculum that meets the needs of a diverse group of students. Given the diverse and changing population of students in urban schools, questions about what and how to teach, and how to assess progress, are constants. Creating a curriculum that draws on the life experiences of the child takes time away from preparing them to pass the standardized tests, for example. Balancing the curriculum so that all voices are heard, not just the dominant voices, is another. Wanting to reward students for their creativity and good effort, on the one hand, and yet needing to be clear with them about how they do or do not meet the academic standards of the class at the same time, is a third. Whereas the details of these dilemmas, as well as the details of all of the dilemmas discussed in the book, will be different from one to the next, we can begin to see that there are predictable categories of dilemmas within which common characteristics exist.

Our consideration of Schwab's (1983) fourth "commonplace" milieu also adds to the predictability of the dilemmas facing teachers and their ability to manage them effectively. Schwab's attention to milieu high-lights the importance of context in both anticipating and understanding the work of teaching. Teaching dilemmas, like teaching itself, are context specific, in spite of the push in the United States currently toward stan-dardization that suggests that teaching approaches that work with chil-dren in Boise, Idaho, will work with children in Oakland, California. We must argue for high standards for all students in all contexts. But as far as standardization is concerned, we hold a different point of view. We argue instead that the context within which teaching occurs matters in terms of what and how to teach, and what the challenges will be for each. Each context will raise particular challenges for which teachers can anticipate and thus prepare. Our focus has been on the urban context and the kinds of dilemmas teachers can expect to encounter there.

As an example, we considered the factor of poverty that affects high numbers of urban children and youth. In considering Ida's narrative (Chapter 1) we saw how poverty in combination with cultural disciplin-ary differences between the teacher and the student's mother intersected to create a dilemma for Ida, whose student Sharon did not wear her jacket to school. Sharon's mother decided to not let Sharon wear her jacket as punishment for forgetting it so frequently. Ida wondered if she should go against Sharon's mother's wishes and let Sharon borrow a jacket so she would not be cold at school.

Josie's student Bianca provides another example (Chapter 3). Because her family did not have the resources to live otherwise, Bianca shared a very small apartment with her mother and her mother's boyfriend. The stress from living in cramped quarters was exacerbated by their being undocumented, which limited significantly their ability to change the stressful circumstances that affected Bianca's success in school and complicated further Josie's decision about how to act in her best interest. Identifying the characteristics of the context within which teachers choose to teach is an important step in preparing oneself for the predictable teaching dilemmas that will arise there.

SHARING DILEMMAS OF PRACTICE

Reasoning through the dilemmas presented in this book provides the readers an opportunity to practice the skills associated with managing teaching dilemmas. One way to consider the dilemmas presented here is as stories of practice that reveal through their details various teaching challenges that left the teacher-authors uncertain about how to act in the best interest of their students. Reading the dilemmas that way highlights the details of the teaching events, thus, rendering the work of teaching appropriately complex. In many accounts of teaching, the details are left out and the work simplified such that for teachers, the accounts lack believability. For their details alone these dilemmas are important. They document the complexity of the work and suggest, therefore, what teachers need to know, believe, and be able to do to do it well.

Another way to read these stories of practice is to focus on the dilemma itself and consider it in a more universal way as an instance of a broader teaching phenomenon. Consider, for example, Karina, whose dilemma narrative described her students' resistance to the curriculum she planned for them (Chapter 4). We might think of Karina's dilemma as an instance of managing student resistance. Karina is a teacher deeply committed to teaching a rich multicultural curriculum in her 9th-grade social studies class. She is also a teacher deeply committed to welcoming all voices (including student voices) into her classroom—and drawing on those voices as she decides what to teach. Karina's dilemma arose when these two values came into conflict. Her dilemma is an example of students resisting what teachers think is in their best interest. Whereas teachers reading Karina's dilemma case might not be teaching 9th grade or social studies, they will undoubtedly face resistance from some students when they take steps to open the curriculum and teach things that are new to students, or are in some ways different from what the students want or expect. For example, imagine a 3rd-grade teacher who is concerned about the cliques that are forming in her class and decides to address the problem by creating mixed-race, mixed-gender groups of students to do a science project. The intensity of her enthusiasm for this arrangement is met only by a similar intensity of resistance to the idea of her students who want to do the science work with their "regular" friends. This 3rd-grade teacher faces a dilemma caused by student resistance. Though the setting, circumstances, and details are different, the dilemma is similar in kind to Karina's dilemma. Both are dilemmas brought about by student resistance.

Thinking of the dilemma as an instance of a teaching phenomenon is another way to begin to manage them effectively. As we face any particular situation we can ask ourselves "What is this dilemma an example of?" or "What dilemmas have I considered that are like the one I am facing here?" which will put us on the path to reasoning through the current dilemma toward an appropriate action. In considering these dilemmas as instances of a predictable teaching phenomenon, we must keep in mind that most teaching dilemmas are instances of not only one phenomenon of the rich and complex work that teachers do. We have considered Karina's dilemma as an instance of student resistance. It could also be seen as an instance of misjudging student interest or needs. Karina was set to teach an elective titled "Cultures and Identities." She assumed that since her students elected to take the class, they would be open to studying a broad range of cultural identities and that her broad-ranging curriculum would meet their needs. It did not take her long to realize that her conception of what motivated the students to take this class and their actual motivations for doing so were different. Rather than seeing the situation as one of student resistance, she might have turned the spotlight on herself and her misunderstanding of what motivated the students to be in the class in the first place.

Reframing Karina's dilemma slightly from being one of student resistance to one of misunderstanding student interests and needs opens new possibilities for Karina to address the situation. Rather than battling against her students' resistance, she could have built into her plans for teaching an elective class in the future a way of collecting information from her students about why they are taking the course. This would have allowed her to tailor her curriculum to better address their interests and concerns, while at the same time holding onto her commitments, values, and ideas about what she wanted to teach. Reframing dilemmas in this way adds an additional strategy for managing them.

LEARNING FROM THE PRACTICE OF OTHERS

An important premise about learning from experience is that teachers can learn not only from their own experiences but also from the experiences of others. It is with this idea of learning from the experiences of others that I have presented the dilemma cases in this book. Those considered here offer the reader the opportunity to reason through similar and predictable dilemmas—different versions of which they will undoubtedly encounter in their own practice. The book opened with a dilemma faced by Ruth whose student Carlito told a story that Ruth found worrisome. Given that this was the first time Carlito had done any schoolwork at all, Ruth was reluctant to comment on the content of his story for fear of shutting him down. By grappling alongside Ruth as she reasoned through this dilemma, we had the opportunity to witness and participate ourselves in the kind of professional and moral deliberation that is required to manage the dilemmas of teaching. In this way we can learn from Ruth's practice just as we can learn from our own.

The hope is that this process of reasoning through the dilemmas of practice alongside the teacher authors whose work is included in the book offers the opportunity to undo some of the isolation that is endemic to our profession. Teaching is structured in many ways to separate teachers from one another and make sharing their struggles a rare occurrence at best. As we recognize how familiar these cases seem in spite of their being from a different place and, maybe, time, we can begin to see ourselves as members of a community of professionals committed to making a difference in the lives of children who live in urban settings and go to urban schools. The authors of the dilemma narratives discussed in the book are our colleagues, struggling with many of the same dilemmas we are facing today and will face tomorrow. By sharing their work they have helped us build a community of teachers who are better prepared to manage the predictable dilemmas of teaching. This is one instance in teaching when we can be sure that our action—learning together—is in the best interest of the students we serve.

Notes

Chapter 1

1. Novice teachers enrolled in a masters program in California are the authors of the case narratives reviewed in this book. With the exception of the case authors who requested their names be used as authors, all names and places are pseudonyms. The case narratives themselves are true accounts of practice as experienced by the author. The descriptions in the book are a combination of their work and my interpretation of it.

Chapter 2

1. The SAT 9 test that Rosa had to take is no longer given to students in California. At the time parents were able to petition to have their children exempt from taking the test. Whereas Laura was not aware of this option before the testing began, she wondered even after she knew about it whether it was a good idea to have Spanish speaking students opt out. She was concerned that if all second language learners opted out of the test, the school test results would not provide an accurate picture of the learning needs of the school's diverse student population.

Chapter 3

1. This quote was taken from a paper written by Sarah Sugarman for a class I teach titled "Inquiry Into the Teaching Process: Practice Into Theory." This course is the follow-up to the "Introduction to the Profession" class, which was the source of the case dilemmas. The paper was about a series of dilemmas Sarah faced in teaching her student Ricky. After completing the inquiry class, Sarah submitted her paper to *The New Educator*, which is where it was published in 2010.

2. For the full poem see, Nikki Giovanni's "Nikki-Rosa" from *Black Feeling, Black Talk, Black Judgment*. Copyright © 1968, 1970 by Nikki Giovanni. HarperCollins Publishers.

Chapter 4

1. An earlier analysis of Rosella's case appeared in a paper I wrote with my colleague Colette Rabin. The paper, which we presented at the American Educational Research Association (AREA) in 2007, was titled Preparing Teachers to Identify and Respond to the Ethical Dimensions of Race and Racism in Teaching.

Chapter 5

1. California and other states have implemented a rigorous plan of continuous testing in order to ensure equity of instruction and learning opportunities for all children thus leading to better overall academic achievement. The state requires students to take standardized tests every year from grades 2 through 11. They are part of the Standardized Testing and Reporting Program (STAR), which includes the California Standards Tests (CSTs), which is a series of standards-based assessments that include as well the California Modified Assessment (CMA) for students with individualized educational programs and the California Alternate Performance Assessment (CAPA) for students with significant cognitive disabilities who are unable to take the CST or CMA. In addition, in order to graduate high school students must pass the California High School Exit Examination (CAHSEE). Using the scores from the STAR program and the CAHSEE, the state rates each school from 200 to 1,000 on an academic performance index (API). These performance scores, which are for comparison purposes throughout the state, are given to both schools and various subgroups of students within schools. Based on the scores, schools are assigned APT growth targets. (Great Schools, Testing in California: An Overview, 2011)

Reaching those target goals has consequences for the school both in terms of funding limitations and increased regulation. The reality of the challenges faced by many children and their teachers in the urban setting—poverty, lack of adequate resources for urban schools that result in underprepared students, and language differences—render this extensive system of testing debilitating for many teachers and students in urban schools.

References

American Psychological Association. (2011). Effects of poverty, hunger and homelessness on children and youth. Retrieved from http://www.apa.org/pi/families/poverty.aspx

Ballenger, C. (1992). Because you like us: The language of control. *Harvard Educational Review, 62*(2), 199–208.

Banks, J., Cochran-Smith, M., Moll, L., Richert, A., Zeichner, K., LePage, P., & McDonald, M. (2005). Teaching diverse learners. In *Preparing teachers for a changing world: What teachers should learn and be able to do* (pp. 232–274). San Francisco, CA: Jossey-Bass.

Beijaard, D., Meijer, P. C., & Verloop, N. (2004). Reconsidering research on teachers' professional identity. *Teaching and Teacher Education, 20,* 107–128.

Berliner, D. (2009). *Poverty and potential: Out-of-school factors and school success.* Retrieved from http://epicpolicy.org/publication/poverty-and-potential

Burbules, N. C. (1997). Teaching and the tragic sense of education. In N. C. Burbules & D. Hans (Eds.), *Teaching and its predicaments* (pp. 65–78). Boulder, CO: Westview Press.

Caldas, S., & Bankston, C. (1997). Effect of school population socioeconomic status on individual academic achievement. *Journal of Educational Research, 90*(5), 269–277.

Children's Defense Fund. (2010). *The state of America's children.* Retrieved from http://www.childrensdefense.org/child-research-data-publications/data/state-of-americas-children.pdf

Cisneros, S. (1984). *The house on mango street.* New York, NY: Vintage Books.

Cremin, L. (1964). *The transformation of the school: Progressivism in American education, 1876–1957.* New York, NY: Vintage Books.

Cuban, L. (2001). *How can I fix it? Finding solutions and managing dilemmas, an educator's road map.* New York: Teachers College Press.

Delpit, L. (1995). *Other people's children: Cultural conflict in the classroom.* New York, NY: New Press.

Dewey, J. (1902). *The child and the curriculum.* Chicago, IL: University of Chicago Press.

Enyedy, N., Goldberg, J., & Muir W. (2005). Complex dilemmas of identity and practice. *Science Education, 90*(1), 68–93.

Florio-Ruane, S. (2002). More light: An argument for complexity in studies of teaching and teacher education. *Journal of Teacher Education, 53*(3), 203–215.

Ford, J. (2009). *The hotel on the corner of bitter and sweet.* New York, NY: Ballantine Books.

Friedman, M. S. (1960). *Martin Buber: The life of dialogue.* New York, NY: Harper.

Gonzáles, N., Moll, L., & Amanti, C. (2005). *Funds of knowledge: Theorizing practices in households, communities, and classrooms.* Mahwah, NJ: Erlbaum.

Great Schools. (2011). *Testing in California: An overview.* Retrieved from http://www.greatschools.org/students/local-facts-resources/426-testing-in-CA.gs

Hammerness, K., & Matsko, K. K. (2010, April). *What's urban about urban teacher preparation: A case study of the University of Chicago urban teacher education program.* Paper presented at the annual meeting of the American Education Research Association, Denver, CO.

Hawkins, D. (2002). *The informed vision: Essays on learning and human nature.* New York, NY: Algora Press.

Hayslip, L. L., & Wurts, J. (2003). *When heaven and earth changed places.* New York, NY: Penguin.

Herrenkohl, T., Maguin, E., Hill, K., Hawkins, J. D., Abbot, D., & Catalano, R. (2000). Developmental risk factors for youth violence. *Journal of Adolescent Health, 26*(3), 176–186.

Holland, D., Lachicotte, W., Skinner, D., & Cain, C. (2001). *Identity and agency in social worlds.* Cambridge, MA: Harvard University Press.

Horn, I. S., Nolen, S. B., Ward, C., & Campbell, S. S. (2008). The role of identity in learning to teach. *Teacher Education Quarterly, 35*(3), 61–72.

Howard, G. R. (1999). *We can't teach what we don't know: White teachers, multiracial schools.* New York, NY: Teachers College Press.

Howell, J. C. & Decker, S. H. (1999). The youth gangs, drugs, and violence connection. *Juvenile Justice Bulletin.* U.S. Department of Justice, Office of Juvenile Justice and Delinquency Prevention. Washington, DC.

Kozol, J. (1991). *Savage inequalities.* New York, NY: Crown.

Kleibard, H. (1995). *The struggle for the American curriculum, 1893–1958.* New York, NY: Routledge.

LaBoskey, V. K. (2004). The methodology of self-study and its theoretical underpinnings. In J. Loughran, M. L. Hamilton, V. K. LaBoskey, & T. Russell (Eds.), *International handbook of self-study of teaching and teacher education practices* (pp. 817–869). Dordrecht, Netherlands: Kluwer.

Ladson-Billings, G. (1994). *The dreamkeepers: Successful teachers of African American children.* San Francisco, CA: Jossey-Bass.

Ladson-Billings, G. (2001). *Crossing over to Canaan: The journey of new teachers in diverse classrooms.* San Francisco, CA: Jossey-Bass.

Lampert, M. (1985). How do teachers manage to teach? Perspectives on problems in practice. *Harvard Educational Review, 55*(2), 178–194.

Lave, J. (1996). Teaching as learning in practice. *Mind, Culture and Activity, 3,* 149–164.

Lawrence, S. (1997). Beyond race awareness: White racial identity and multiracial teaching. *Journal of Teacher Education, 48*(2), 108–117.

Lee, C. D. (2007). *Culture, literacy, and learning: Taking bloom in the midst of the whirlwind.* New York, NY: Teachers College Press.

Lortie, D. C. (1975). *Schoolteacher: A sociological study.* Chicago, IL: University of Chicago Press.

McDonald, J. (1992). *Teaching: Making sense of an uncertain craft.* New York, NY: Teachers College Press.

Mead, G. H. (1964). *Mind, self and society from the standpoint of a social behaviorist.* Chicago, IL: University of Chicago Press.

Moll, L. E. (2000). Inspired by Vygotsky: Ethnographic experiments in education. In C. D. Lee & P. Smagorinsky (Eds.), *Vygotskian perspectives on literacy research: Constructing meaning through collaborative inquiry* (pp. 256–268). Cambridge, UK: Cambridge University Press.

Noguera, P. (1995). Preventing and producing violence: A critical analysis of responses to school violence. *Harvard Educational Review, 65*(2), 189–213.

Noguera, P. (2003). *City schools and the American dream: Reclaiming the promise of public education.* New York, NY: Teachers College Press.

Oakes, J., & Lipton, M. (2003). *Teaching to change the world.* New York, NY: McGraw-Hill.

Olsen, B. (2008). How reasons for entry into the profession illuminate teacher identity development. *Teacher Education Quarterly, 35*(3), 23–40.

Orfield, G., & Lee, C. (2005). Why segregation matters: Education and inequality. *The Civil Rights Project.* Cambridge, MA: Harvard University.

Palmer, P. (1998). *The courage to teach.* San Francisco, CA: Jossey-Bass.

Popham, W. J. (2001). *The truth about testing: An educator's call to action.* Alexandria, VA: Association for Supervision and Curriculum Development.

Ravitch, D. (2010). The death and life of the great American school system: How testing and choice are undermining education. New York, NY: Basic Books.

Richert, A. E., Donahue, D. M., & LaBoskey, V. K. (2009). Preparing White teachers to teach in a racist nation: What do they need to know and be able to do? In W. Ayers, T. Quinn, & D. Stovall (Eds.), *Handbook of social justice education,* 640–653. Mahwah, NJ: Erlbaum.

Ronfeldt, M., & Grossman, P. (2008). Becoming a professional: Experimenting with possible selves in professional preparation. *Teacher Education Quarterly, 35*(3), 41–60.

Schwab, J. (1983). The practical 4: Something for curriculum professors to do. *Curriculum Inquiry, 13*(3), 239–265.

Sugarman, S. (2008). Looking Deep: Finding Funds of Knowledge for Ethical Teaching. Unpublished manuscript prepared for the Inquiry into Teaching class, Mills College.

Sugarman, S. (2010). Seeing past the fences: Finding funds of knowledge for ethical teaching. *The New Educator, 6*(2), 96–117.

Tatum, B. (2007). *Can we talk about race? And other conversations.* Boston, MA: Beacon Press.

The state of America's children yearbook: A report from the Children's Defense Fund. (2010). Retrieved from http://www.childrensdefense.org/child-research-data-publications/data/state-of-americas-children-2010-report.html

Vygotsky, L. (1978). *Mind in society.* Cambridge, MA: Harvard University Press.

Wenger, E. (1998). *Communities of practice: Learning, meaning, and identity.* New York, NY: Cambridge University Press.

Wiesel, E. (1972). *Night.* New York, NY: Hill & Wang.

Zirkel, S. (2008). The influence of multicultural educational practices on student outcomes and intergroup relations. *Teachers College Record, 110*(6), 1147–1181.

Zumwalt, K., & Craig, E. (2005). Teachers' characteristics: Research on the demographic profile. In M. Cochran-Smith & K. M. Zeichner (Eds.), *Studying teacher education* (pp. 111–156). Malwah, NJ: Erlbaum.

Dilemma Authors

Taylor Albright
Laura Alvarez
Lizzy Hull Barnes
Rebecca Bearg
Emily Creed Brunick
Erica Bryant
Rachel Curtin
Emma Godinez Elphick
Juliet Spear Gardner
Shannon Hand

Lisa Holmes
Erica Hutter
Jessica Lopez-Tello
Suzanne Motley
Sara Norris
Rebecca Pollack
Sarah Sugarman
Ines Trinh
Leora Wolf-Prussan

Index

Josie's Dilemma, 43–46, 106

Karina's Dilemma, 59–62, 69,
    72–73, 75, 107–108
Kleibard, H., 62–63
Knowledge of students' situations
    and needs, 8–14, 41–49
    assessment dilemmas, 89–97,
    100–102
Kozol, J., 11, 26

LaBoskey, V. K., 35, 70
Lachicotte, W., 21
Ladson-Billings, G., 13–14
Lampert, M., 6
Language and language barriers.
    See also English language
    learners (ELL); Immigrant
    students
    assessment dilemmas, 81–85,
    89–93
    identity and, 26–30
    multiplicity of, 34
    Spanish language, 30–34
    subjective grading and, 92–93
Late submission of assignments,
    93–97, 100–102
Latina/o students
    assessment dilemmas, 89–93
    curriculum dilemmas, 73–75
Laura's Dilemma, 22–25, 34, 37,
    85, 111
Lave, J., 79
Lawrence, S., 72
Learning, connection between
    assessment and, 79–80
Learning disabilities, students
    with, 47
Lee, C., 9

Lee, C. D., 12, 13–14, 30
Legal obligations, 45
LePage, P., 11
Lipton, M., 26, 62–63, 79–80, 85,
    88
Lopez-Tello, J., 117
Lortie, D. C., 21
Lucy's Dilemma, 18–20, 25, 34,
    36–37
Luella's Dilemma, 89–93, 96

Maguin, E., 56
Management of teaching
    dilemmas, 4–17
Mathematics classes, 89–93
Matsko, K. K., 26
McDonald, J., 8
McDonald, M., 11
Mead, G. H., 21
Meijer, P. C., 21
Mid-year introduction of student,
    81–85
Middle school settings
    curriculum dilemmas, 73–75
    professional identity dilemmas,
    26–30
    student-teacher relationship
    dilemmas, 53–57
Misha's Dilemma, 77–78
Mitigation of uncertainty in
    teaching, 104–107
Moll, L., 11, 13–14
Moll, L. E., 30
Moral aspect of teachers'
    professional responsibility,
    101–102
Motley, S., 117
Muir W., 20
Multiple choice tests, 87–88

About the Author

Anna Ershler Richert is a professor at the School of Education at Mills College in Oakland, California where she is also Director of the Master of Arts in Education with an Emphasis on Teaching (MEET) Program. She is Faculty Director of the Mills Teacher Scholars Program that supports the inquiry practice of more than 100 Bay Area teachers. In her job as a Mills faculty member she has spent over two decades preparing teachers to teach in urban schools, while also learning from them what is entailed in doing this work. She is a member and frequent presenter for the American Education Research Association and a past recipient of the Rockefeller Foundation Bellagio Fellowship where she began the project that resulted in this book.